HOW TO
Raise a Puppy
YOU CAN LIVE WITH

New, Revised Second Edition

Clarice Rutherford
David H. Neil, M.R.C.V.S.

Alpine Publications Inc.

Library of Congress Cataloging-in-Publication Data

Rutherford, Clarice.
    How to raise a puppy you can live with / by Clarice Rutherford and David H. Neil. — 2nd ed.
        p.   cm.
    Includes bibliographical references and index.
    ISBN 0-931866-57-X : $9.95
    1. Puppies—Training. 2. Puppies—Behavior. 3. Puppies.
    4. Dogs—Training. 5. Dogs—Behavior. 6. Dogs.   I. Neil,
    David H.   II. Title.
    SF431.R87   1992
    636.7'0887—dc20   92-9723
                                                                          CIP
Printed in the United States of America

Second Edition
    2   3   4   5   6   7   8   9

ISBN: 0-931866-57-X

Cover Design: Diane Burkhardt
Cover Photo: © Walter Chandoha, 1992

TO ALL THE PUPPY PEOPLE
WHO HAVE MADE A CHOICE

A Contract

I have chosen to share my life with you, a member of another species. I pledge to appreciate your uniqueness as a member of the canine family and to attempt to raise you and discipline you in terms of this uniqueness. In return, I know that you will do your best to fit into my life-style if it is caninely possible and will reciprocate my attentions to you by letting me share your view of the universe. I will also be a better person for having this experience. I hope your life will be better for having been with me.

CONTENTS

INTRODUCTION

"If the status quo prevails, dog ownership is going to get tougher, and deservedly so . . . The way we play it may have very significant impact on the future of the domestic dog in urban society."

Throughout the remarkable history of animal domestication, the relationship that has evolved between man and dog is by far the most ancient, and it has become the most intimate. Man and dog, in fact, have evolved together, each contributing to the survival of the other.

Every year, countless numbers of people develop relationships with their dogs in work and play, allowing subtle, effective two-way communication to be comfortably established. In some of these relationships, the bond continues to grow stronger, and what begins as a matter of expediency between two awkward strangers — the new owner and the new puppy dog — becomes, in the fullness of time, a meeting of minds and hearts.

It is generally thought that the domestic dog is a descendant of the wolf, retaining many of its characteristics. One of these is the ability to live together in packs. The wolf pack has a definite order of seniority, the most senior animal of all being the pack leader. The dog is focused on the human group or family. Just as we recognize hierarchy in our families, the dog naturally fits into this also and sees its owner as the pack leader.

At the dawn of civilization in the ancient city of Jericho, there were dogs as large as wolves and as small as terriers. Already man had selected and bred different types of dogs for different functions. This selecting and breeding has continued for thousands of years as a continuous process. We now have many breeds of dog that have been developed to perform many specific roles to help us in our day-to-day activities, in work and at leisure.

The twentieth century has seen the amazing adaptation of various breeds to become seeing-eye and hearing-ear dogs. Dogs also assist the severely physically handicapped in wheelchairs. No matter what function dogs perform, the basic underlying theme throughout the vast majority of them is *companionship*.

Pet dogs in contemporary society continue to provide a focus of attention and affection for people who feel very much alone, whether confined to their homes or to an institutional setting. During the 1980s, much attention was redirected toward the dog as a social facilitator in our society. Those of you who grew up with a family dog know only too well the positive contribution that your dog made to that sometimes difficult process.

Having praised dogs to the skies, however, we recognize that all is not well with the unwritten contract between man and dog. In our introduction to the 1981 edition of this book, we referred to the growing concern with dog problems and to the efforts to severely restrict or prevent dog ownership.

Too many dogs do not enjoy a healthy family situation and get into so much trouble that they are either impounded or are relinquished to the animal shelter. Meanwhile, the dog population continues to rise. In 1990, the dog population was estimated at 55 million, and reliable authorities on pet population dynamics estimate that by the year 2000, this figure may have risen to 66 million. It has been estimated that the number of dogs put to sleep each year reaches 6 million, and possibly quite a lot higher. Will this figure increase as the dog population increases? It may well.

It was recently stated by a seasoned and well-informed observer of the problem that most of these animals were approximately eighteen months old and, having outgrown their cuteness, were having behavioral problems that their owners could not deal with.

As active members of our humane society in Larimer County, Colorado, in the 1970s, we were only too well aware of this problem, and it was a major motivator for us to buckle down and write this book. We believe that the first step toward getting a dog that you and everyone else can live with — after selecting the right breed, of course — is to find a good breeder who recognizes how important the first two months of a puppy's life are in determining how he will be able to deal with the big world as a mature dog. When your carefully selected puppy comes home with you, you are now in the driver's seat, and your knowledge and patient actions will further determine whether you will soon own a dog that you — and your community — can live with.

We believe that everything can be accomplished by the use of praise and contingent reward, which includes the initial use of tidbits. We have had little or no use for push-pull-slap methods, and in this new edition of our book, we emphasize positive reinforcement even more, based on the experience of our readers and of ourselves over the last ten years.

In 1981, we appealed to dog breeders, show judges, fanciers, trialists, moms, dads, and kids to unite in forming a knowledgeable, expert, and caring front to get well-adjusted dogs back as the predominant representatives of the species. Well, we all have a long way to go yet, dear friends, but your response has been heartwarming. We have had a lot of valuable feedback, and it has helped shape this edition. Special thanks to our more than 100,000 readers of the first edition for confirming that the book works.

Once again, we are in debt to all of those authors who contributed to our earlier education, particularly John Paul Scott, John L. Fuller, Michael Fox, Clarence J. Pfaffenberger, Leon F. Whitney, William E. Campbell, Daniel F. Tortora, Ian Dunbar, and Job Michael Evans. The influence of Benjamin Hart and Victoria Voith in the veterinary literature was invaluable.

One of the big questions in the 1990s concerns raising a normal puppy when during the day the entire household is either out to work or at school. We are especially indebted to our dear friend and inveterate dog lover, Dr. Suzanne Hetts, who studied this in detail at Colorado State University with Dr. Phil Lehner. She gave us more confidence in workable strategies to prepare puppies for a place in a family with this life-style. We also express a deep appreciation to Barbera Curtis for her years of involvement in our development of a successful puppy kindergarten course. Special thanks go to Sandy Whicker, and to Steve and Sue Henning, for their insights into puppy behavior, puppy evaluations, and puppy socialization. Discussions with them are always vigorous and thought provoking, and in this way, they have contributed much to this book.

CHAPTER 1

CHOOSING YOUR PUPPY

"Do not yield to the temptation of considering only the kind of dog you loved as a kid. A big Saint Bernard, for example, might not fit your life in the city at all."

When you're looking at a litter of little puppies that are so easy to handle and to control, it's easy to overlook the thought that within a few months these puppies will have the size and general behavioral characteristics of their breed, together with individual behavioral tendencies inherited from the parents. Unfortunately, when you select one of them and take him home, you might be unhappy with the result, because that little puppy can change into a much larger and more vigorous dog than your home and life-style can manage. It's not the pup's fault that you didn't carefully give some thought to the adult dog into which that pup would grow.

1

The best puppy for you is the one that will grow up into the right dog for you. In choosing a puppy, you have to be able to visualize what the adult dog will be like physically and behaviorally, and how he will fit into your home facilities, as well as into your life. For instance, a person who would be very content with the relatively slow-moving Bassett would probably be frustrated with a very quick-moving, high-energy terrier. The sheepdog that you grew up with back on the farm — so much a part of your life then, and about which you have so many happy memories — may be totally unsuited to your current sophisticated urban environment, with strictly limited time outdoors.

In choosing the right dog for your future, you are planning a relationship that hopefully will endure for many happy years until "death do you part." It makes a bit of sense, then, to make your choice wisely. To do this, you have to reflect on your own personality and life-style and see if a dog fits in there somewhere. If you feel that it does, then you next have to choose what kind of dog you want — and this is where some of you may need a bit of help.

In the past, many of us would inevitably have acquired a dog very quickly, perhaps relying more on a whim than on good judgment. Some of us were lucky, but as we suggested in the introduction, a fair few of us were not. Perhaps the first deliberate action in acquiring a puppy is to set aside sufficient time to familiarize yourself with all that the world of dogs can offer you, and, in turn, what you can offer a dog. During this time, you can resort to the abundant literature on dogs and seek expert advice. In this way, you start to zero-in on that special little chap that will so enrich your life in the future. Chances are he hasn't even been born yet!

A puppy's adult personality will be shaped by a combination of three factors — his breed, his individual genetic behavior, and the socialization that he receives during the first four months of life. Breed characteristics are generalizations, of course, but they are recognizable in most members of each particular breed. It's obvious to the observant person that different breeds not only look different, but behave differently.

For example, Huskies and Malamutes are very leader oriented. They need to know at all times that you're the leader or they'll quickly start doing things their way. Terriers are born convinced of their own importance. Sheepdogs need much outdoor activity or they can become irritable. Scent hounds such as the Beagle and the Bloodhound are quite independent and are led by their noses, while sight hounds such as the Afghan and the Greyhound tend to be aloof and easily distracted by distant movements to the extent of running off. Both types of hounds generally do not display their affection by trying to please their owners but still have their own charm, which is very appealing to some people. The guard dogs such as Rottweilers, Pinschers, and German Shepherds need a firm attitude, but when they are given sensible, consistent training, they are very loyal and dependable. Sporting breeds are often easily excited by numerous sights, sounds, and smells. The miniature breeds are bright and very clever, but because of their size, they are easy to spoil, and then they think that they rule the household. And remember, *all* breeds — large, medium, and small — need exercise, which can be lots of fun if you teach them running and retrieving games. However, they should not be turned loose and allowed to run the neighborhood. That kind of exercise they *don't* need. It's dangerous for the dog and inconsiderate to the neighbors.

You should be sure before acquiring a puppy that his individual personality will be acceptable to you and your family, to your accommodations, and to your life-style. A good source of information about the breed in which you are interested is your local kennel club, which can give you the names of breeders. When buying a puppy, you're not just buying a pedigree — you're buying the expertise, the understanding of the puppy's needs, and the advice that the breeder can give you based on experience with that particular breed.

Another good source of information is to attend a dog show and buy a catalog of the dogs entered. This lists the names and addresses of the people who are showing, and you can follow up by contacting a breeder in your area. If this is not a possible means of contact, *Dog World* magazine is available at many newsstands. This publication lists a large number of breeders to contact nationwide. The American Kennel Club will supply names of local breeders or will give an address for the national breed club. Write to the American Kennel Club, 51 Madison Avenue, New York, NY 10010. In Canada, write to the Canadian Kennel Club, 2150 Bloor Street West, Toronto, Ontario, M6S 4V7.

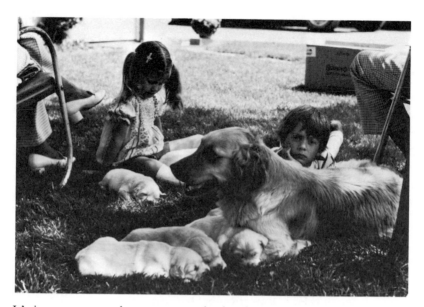

It's important to select a puppy who has been well-socialized.

Read as much as you can about the history of the breed and about the behavioral traits, and talk with other owners if possible before you finally decide which breed to select. Expect the breeder to question you about your life-style and about the plans that you have for your dog. Good breeders care about making sure that the puppy goes to a suitable home. This can help you in your breed selection. Then, buy wisely from breed experts who have a reputation to maintain.

We cannot recommend buying puppies that are born in puppy mills (usually sold in pet stores). The buyer cannot learn anything about the parents of the puppy and knows nothing about the treatment that the puppy received during the sensitive stages of birth to eight weeks, nor about hidden health problems. The soundness of your pup (freedom from inherited diseases, including skeletal abnormalities) can affect the cost of ownership as a result of veterinary bills, or worse, result in the premature loss of your pet.

When you have selected the breed that has a size and disposition best for you, it is time to consider the individual personality that you want your pup to have. A good indication of this is the personality of the parent dogs. Behavior is a hereditary factor, just as are the appearance, the length of coat, or the type of head, and behavior is of greater importance to most buyers. Therefore, if either parent is very shy or very aggressive, you will want to look at other litters before making a choice. Conversely, if the parent dogs like people and are pleasant to be around, you will know that there is a good chance that the pups will have the same qualities. Most breeders are very willing to discuss the breed and individual characteristics of their line of dogs, because the most important part of selling puppies is to see that they go to the most suitable home. The puppy will not be a carbon copy of either parent but will likely have some of the behavioral characteristics of each.

The third aspect of a puppy's personality is the socializing that the pup receives from the breeder and the behavior-molding that the pup receives from his new master. Every breeder knows that careful breeding is only part of the story, although a very important part. Breeders have seen a promising puppy ruined by bad training or simply a lack of training. If a breeder tells you that he doesn't think that a dog is right for you, he often has come to that conclusion through hard experience. So try to find a breed that may be more compatible to your life-style, or defer getting a dog until you really can care for it.

Choosing Your Own Puppy

Selecting a puppy is often a matter of discussing with the breeder which puppy is most likely to fit your life-style. For example, if at seven weeks a Labrador Retriever puppy is running around as fast as it can, grabbing your pant leg, crashing into you when you're down on your knees, jumping up into your face, or grabbing at your hand when you try to pet it, then you can be quite certain that this puppy will be a handful and will do best with an experienced person. Another Labrador puppy in that same litter may be quiet, may come to you slowly at first, and may lick your hand or your face. This pup will be much easier to train, and because he's a Labrador, you know that he will become sufficiently lively when he is acquainted with his new home. Which pup is best for you? Or perhaps you prefer a pup that isn't always fussing for attention. An independent pup that is busy sniffing, not caring whether he's petted, might develop into the type of dog that you would want after you have bonded to each other.

Breeders who have been involved with their breed for a considerable length of time develop a sharp eye from experience. They become familiar with the behavioral tendencies of the bloodlines within the breed, and with how the puppy's reactions will translate into later behavior in adult dogs. They also can see behavioral qualities that are not testable, such as that extra spark of "smarts" or charisma.

Another situation that often exists with a breeder who has puppies that are reserved ahead of time is that each person gets a pick. For example, you might have the third-pick female because two people reserved a pup before you did. Another person might have fourth-pick male. It might seem that you won't get the puppy that is best for you, but it's amazing how the pups seem to go to the right home. The fourth pick in a litter that is carefully planned for temperament may be better than the first pick in a poorly planned litter. Also, the "pick" criteria may be different from yours for each of those selecting ahead of you. Many breeders use puppy testing and their own evaluation to match each puppy with the appropriate owner.

Puppy temperament testing is used by many breeders as one method of evaluating their puppies. They want to see if the pups conform to the evaluation that they have developed in their known daily observations of the pups. To be effective, the test must be given the same to each puppy or the scoring is invalid. The evaluation of the scoring should be done by an experienced person and should preferably include previous observations of the puppy. Under these conditions, the test is a good tool to use.

If you saw your puppy's litter around six weeks of age, you probably noticed differences in temperament when the pups were playing together. However, observation of the pups with their littermates can sometimes give a false impression of the pup's innate desire to please and to adjust to people. A puppy should never be selected based on his behavior with his littermates. He should be removed from the litter and played with individually. Observations made by an inexperienced buyer on only one visit may not accurately reflect the true puppy — the hell raiser might be tired, and the wall flower may have just awakened and may be feeling his oats! Observations over several visits, the breeder's opinions, and testing will give a better rounded picture and may prevent unfortunate pairings.

Perhaps you will have the pick between two or three puppies. Carry the puppies, one at a time, away from the litter, far enough so that the pup can't see or hear his littermates. Is the pup curious, wagging his tail, and exploring? Is he worried and trying to return to the litter? Can you attract his attention by clapping your hands, or by bending down close to him and having him run to you? Does he follow you when you walk past him and coax him? Does the pup look at you when you hold him close and talk to him? The final decision on your part might be an emotional one, but part of that selection process is based on how you react to the puppy on a one-to-one basis. The puppy that you *don't* want is the shy pup that wants to run and hide or the aggressive puppy that nips at you when you try to play with him.

When You Can't Visit the Litter

You'll have to trust the breeder. Ask all the same questions initially, and ask about the observations that you would make if you could see the litter. Tell the breeder the type of puppy you want, then rely on the breeder to make the final decision. You can certainly ask for references and contact previous buyers.

Many breeders require a deposit if you want a puppy held for you. The remaining payment is made when you pick up the puppy, or just before shipping. You should receive the puppy litter registration at this time, or a written promise that it soon will be in the mail.

The Best Age to Acquire A Puppy

A large number of breeders consider seven weeks to be the ideal age for a puppy to leave his littermates and go to his new home. Others prefer to keep their puppies in the litter until ten weeks of age. It is advisable for the buyer to be guided by the experience of the breeder. The main concern for the new owner is to be certain that the pup has received sufficient individual attention and puppy training from the breeder since the age of six weeks.

The Older Puppy

If you are considering a puppy that is twelve weeks or older, you need to get two assurances from the breeder. First, the puppy must have been taken out of his pen on a regular basis to experience different environments; otherwise, kennel shyness may develop. Second, the puppy must have spent time alone with a person on a regular basis (for example, fifteen minutes a day, four days a week); if not, his socialization will be retarded, and much time and effort will be necessary to bring the pup to a normal attitude toward people and other dogs. If these two aspects have been taken care of by the breeder — in other words, if the puppy training has begun — you can do just fine by buying an older puppy.

Don't Bring Home Two

If two puppies are desired, wait until the first pup is five to six months old before bringing home the second. By this time, the pup will have bonded to you and will be comfortable spending more time alone in his yard or house area. The problem with littermates is that the intial bonding is to each other rather than to you. If they have each other, neither pup will give you his full attention. This makes training almost impossible. Modern research in dog behavior indicates that puppy-human bonding is essential to a superior relationship. It's a very rare person who can induce bonding by having more than one puppy at a time.

Other Considerations

Unfortunately, some individuals raise puppies only for what financial gain they might experience, and they care nothing about the needs of the puppies. Don't hesitate to ask for specific information. Get a detailed report of what care and activities have been done with the puppies, and find out how knowledgeable the person is about the characteristics and history of the breed. If the breeder seems lacking in any of these areas, don't fall victim to a hard sell. These people should not be encouraged to perpetuate their puppy activities. They do more harm than good for the dog world.

There are many conscientious and reliable breeders who breed and raise puppies with great care. Take the time to find the right one. A good breeder will give you references, will tell you why they did *this* breeding, and will share with you their expectations for the litter. Good breeders will know what problems you're likely to encounter and will have provisions in your contract in case of trouble — either genetic defects or changing home circumstances under which you can't keep the puppy.

We have the advantage of raising and training dogs in a time when much has been discovered about the basic developmental periods of a puppy's life. This is very exciting. We can take what heredity gives us and then control the environment to develop the best possible personality in the adult dog.

Photo by Anita Stewart.

CHAPTER 2

BEHAVIOR:
THE ENVIRONMENTAL FACTOR

Urban living does not come naturally to a dog, but by understanding a puppy's needs, we can help him to adjust.

A major portion of this book pertains to the first six months of a puppy's life with emphasis on the first three months. There's a good reason for this. We believe that these early months are absolutely the key to molding a dog's behavior so that he can fit into the complexities of life in the twentieth century. Let's face it, urban life isn't exactly a natural environment for man's best friend — but with care it can be one to which he can adapt.

Life was great for the dog in small-town America where the family dog went everywhere with the kids and also had his own circle of friends among the other dogs in the neighborhood. In contrast, most dogs today live isolated lives in backyards, pens, or homes, completely at the mercy of a few members of the family who are often very busy with other activities. If the dog is fed every day and has shelter, we are too likely to think that we're filling his needs.

The dog is by nature a pack animal with definite social needs. Through the millenia while man and dog were evolving, the dog developed empathy with humans and a desire for attention from his human pack members. If this need for attention is ignored the dog can become very frustrated and might well begin to indulge in activities like incessant barking and destroying property. If the dog is not only kept in such an environment as an adult, but is bred and raised with inadequate attention, the problem is compounded.

Dog behavior studies have determined that the first twelve weeks of a dog's life are vitally important because a puppy's experiences during this time will affect his emotional responses as an adult dog. It stands to reason, then, that if we know how the puppy is growing and what the puppy needs during these different stages, we can help every puppy get the best possible start in life.

The need for human attention begins shortly after the puppy is born. During the first few weeks of life the pup is going through the most amazing process of growth. At first, his world is dark and silent and consists solely of contact with his littermates and the constant care of his mother. After about two weeks he begins to learn new behaviors which will adapt him well to living in a sensory and social world. By eight weeks of age he has full use of his sensory and motor systems and his central nervous system has reached maturity, ready for whatever learning experiences await.

The puppy's central nervous system, and therefore his behavior, develops in a wondrously particular and precise pattern, and each stage of growth has an effect on the puppy's actions. If the pup doesn't have his physical and social needs satisfied during any one of these periods, certain characteristics of his personality will be stalled at that particular stage of development. This, in turn, will have an effect on how the dog will behave when he is older.

For example, some dogs remain overly suspicious of anything new or different, often because they never developed investigative behavior when it was a normal part of their growing up (eight to

Photo by Deloris Reinke.

twelve weeks). Another dog might be too easily excited, to the extent of appearing hyperactive, as a result of not having had adequate environmental stimulation during the stage of learning how to sort out sounds, sights, and smells (six to ten weeks). And both the shy and the hyperactive personality can be strongly affected by a lack of human contact from three to seven weeks.

You are undoubtedly wondering if knowing about these developmental stages in a puppy's life is all that important. Obviously, many dog owners have raised very fine dogs without such information — for good reasons. These pups may have had outgoing personalities and have been able to overcome some lack of socialization. Even more likely, these pups were fortunate enough to be raised in homes where their needs were automatically and unknowingly met during each period. Dogs have been successfully socialized for more than 10,000 years without anyone being specifically aware of it, let alone labeling the process!

So it is today in many homes. Puppies that get a lot of attention and receive touch, sound, and visual stimulation in the course of a normal day grow up to be healthy, well-adjusted dogs.

But not all puppies are so carefully raised. If the breeder is away from home during the day, for instance, a certain amount of time must be reserved in the evening for puppy activities. This is why timing the arrival of a litter is important. A concerned breeder checks the calendar when planning a breeding to make sure that puppies will not be neglected. If certain social obligations or an unusually heavy work load will occur at a certain time of the year, a litter should not be bred to arrive at such a time.

The breeder who is not willing to give some time to the puppies should let someone else do the breeding and puppy raising. There are enough poorly adjusted dogs in the world now that did not get the people-care they needed while they were puppies.

This is where the so-called "puppy mills" are totally negligent. The people who operate these mills have a large number of female dogs whose only function is to produce puppies for profit and who are often kept isolated in cages, boxes, or other very small areas. This so-called "breeder" has no understanding of the needs of the dog and does not realize the damage done to a pup's personality by giving it no socialization during the first eight weeks. It is not only extreme cruelty to keep the parent dogs in such confining isolation, but it is also cruel to the puppies to deny them the socialization they must have if they are to adjust to living with people as they grow up.

Today, so much has been learned about dog behavior that there is no excuse for a socially maladjusted dog. Whether you are a breeder who is introducing the world of dogs to newcomers, or whether you are a first-time puppy owner, there is much you can do to make this a good world for your pet. You don't have the luxury of many days and weeks to be a partner in your puppy's personality development. But you don't have to give up a normal routine and become a "puppy-recluse" in order to accomplish your goal. Mostly, you just need to be aware of what's going on in the natural process as a newborn puppy grows from a "blob" into a bouncing young adult.

CHAPTER 3

THE DEVELOPMENTAL PERIOD
(The First Three Months)

Experiences during the first three months are the
foundation of the puppy's mature personality.

The first three months of a dog's life are called the developmental months because it is during this time that almost all of the dog's basic behavioral patterns are developed. At least the first seven weeks of the puppy's life are the responsibility of the breeder. Beyond that age, the responsibility for socialization shifts to the new owner. Each period has specific activities that can help a puppy grow emotionally.

There are three basic developmental periods in the first twelve weeks. These periods are defined here by calendar time, but this doesn't mean that all puppies will begin each period on exactly the same day. There will be variances depending upon the breed and upon individual differences within the litter. Littermates usually catch up with each other, however, by the end of the last period.

Table 1. Basic Developmental Periods

Neonatal Period	Transitional Period	Socialization
1-14 days	15-21 days	22-84 days
birth to 2 weeks	2 to 3 weeks	3-12 weeks

In order for us to understand a puppy's needs as he begins to grow, we should become familiar with the characteristics of the different periods. This chapter will cover the general description of each period. Chapter 4 will discuss the breeder's role in raising puppies, and Chapters 5 and 6 will deal with the new owner's activities in taking a puppy to his new home.

The Neonatal Period

1-14 days	Key Puppy Behavior:
	Spends about 90 percent of time sleeping
	Susceptible to excess heat or cold
	Crawls
	Nurses
	Seeks warmth of littermates and mother
	Can usually right himself if turned over
	Needs anal stimulation for urination and defecation

At this stage the bitch is the main influence on the puppy. Her health, milk supply, and attitude toward the pups, and later toward people who come to look at the puppies, will influence the behavioral development of the litter. If she is overly fearful or aggres-

Photo copyright Clifford Oliver.

sive, this can be imprinted on the puppies and their future behavior might be very similar to hers, whether or not they were born with a fearful or aggressive genetic trait. Thus, a behavior can be either genetically or environmentally derived.

At this age, the pup's abilities are confined to sucking, vocalizing, and crawling slowly. The senses of sight and hearing are not functional yet. The eyes may begin to open around ten days of age but in most cases are not open until about fourteen days of age.

The puppy learns about his environment through touch. You can observe him crawling around, moving his head from side to side until he bumps into his mother or a littermate. A puppy might crawl away from the bitch, but she should be able to retrieve him by carrying him in her mouth, providing he doesn't crawl out of her sight or sound. Urination and defecation are reflex responses that occur only when the bitch licks her puppies' anal and genital region.

During this period, the pup is aware only of heat, cold, and pain. He is not yet capable of regulating body heat efficiently and therefore needs his mother and the other puppies to help maintain his own warmth. Even though it looks as though the pups do nothing but eat and sleep, this is a very important period. The central nervous system is rapidly developing, getting ready for the next stage.

The Transitional Period

15-21 days	Key Puppy Behavior:
	Eyes open
	Teeth begin to emerge
	Gets up on four legs and takes a few steps
	Begins to lap liquids
	Defecates without the mother's stimulation

The puppy's eyesight is dim, but he is ready for the next adventure. He discovers that the other pups are more than just warm lumps to be crawled over and slept on. He begins to stagger around on four legs, lifting himself up first on his front legs, then on the hind legs as they become equally strong. Activity periods are brief, followed by sleep to gather strength for the next concentrated effort. By the end of this transitional period, the pup can walk on four legs and lap milk or soft food in a fairly efficient manner (although not very elegantly).

The pup no longer needs constant care from the bitch and is beginning to defecate without her stimulus. He starts to get interested in littermates. The very beginnings of pack-oriented behavior, such as pawing at each others' faces and chewing on littermates' ears, are seen at this stage.

The Socialization Period

Socialization is the name given to the next nine weeks, the growth period lasting from three to twelve weeks of age. We have found that this period can be divided into four stages, each of which is an important stepping-stone for the one that follows.

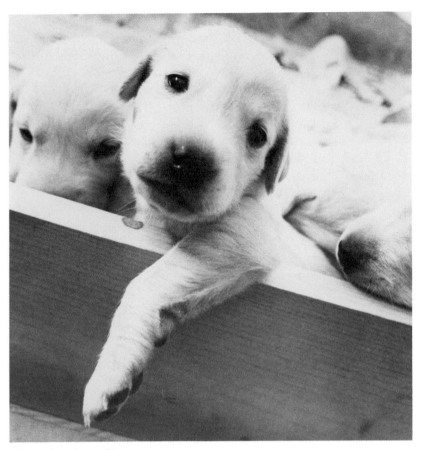

Photo by Janet Yosay.

The dog's primary social relationships develop during this time. If his primary relationships are with people, the pup will be able to form lasting relationships throughout his life, but the puppy that receives little human contact during this time will find it difficult to adjust to humans as long as he lives.

The puppy also needs to be with littermates and the bitch during the first weeks of the socialization period. He needs to learn how to act around other members of his own species, or he could become a dog that picks fights easily or has problems with mating (if this should subsequently be desired).

The Period of Becoming Aware
(First Stage of Socialization)

22-28 days	**Key Puppy Behavior:**
3-4 weeks	Can hear, see, and the sense of smell is becoming much more complex
	Begins to eat food
	Begins to bark, wag tail, and bite other pups
4-5 weeks	Uses legs quite well but tires easily
	Paws
	Bares teeth
	Growls
	Chases
	Plays prey-killing games

We have divided the socialization period into four stages not only for ease of discussion but also because the behavioral patterns of the puppy are readily distinguishable and determined by their physical age. The central nervous system continues to develop rapidly during this time. The puppy now has both sight and hearing ability and by four weeks is beginning to develop perception of distance. The sense of smell, which is one of the first to develop, is now starting to develop a subtlety that becomes such an important part of the perception of the world by the adult dog.

The beginning of the socialization period can be determined for each puppy by using the startle-reaction test. *When a puppy visibly reacts to a loud sound, he is into the socialization stage.* This is also a means of telling which pups are on a slightly different time schedule in their physical development. This is valuable information because otherwise these pups might unjustly be labeled as dull-witted or slow when actually the only problem is that they need time to catch up physically with the others. Puppies, however,

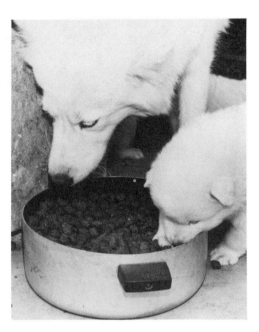

Puppy begins to show
interest in food.
Photo by Deloris Reinke.

don't always go by the book and react on the twenty-first or
twenty-second day. One breeder accidentally dropped a pan about
four feet from the puppies on the eighteenth day and got a big
reaction. On the twenty-first day the puppies didn't react to a loud
noise. By then they apparently accepted it as part of their world.

Even if we didn't look at the calendar or use the startle test, we
would know when this period begins. It's as if someone pushed
the "on" button. Virtually overnight, the puppy turns into an
animated little being.

From twenty-two to twenty-eight days, the puppy is experiencing
a shower of sensory stimulation. So much awareness of the world
around him is happening so suddenly that the pup needs a very
stable home environment to balance the excess stimulation. The
bitch should remain with the litter as much as possible during this
week.

By the end of the third week, the pup displays much more complex behavior than at the beginning of the period, which is an
indication of how rapidly development occurs. The pups now play

During this period the bitch can be separated from her puppies occasionally during the day, but her presence is still important to the puppies. *Photo by Deloris Reinke.*

together. They start to learn how much chewing and biting the other pups will take. They begin to show adult behavior patterns with their play-fighting, scruff-holding, and prey-killing (head-shaking) movements, and they are beginning to bark, growl, and snap at each other. Some pups begin barking and wagging tails around three weeks of age, but this varies with the breed and the individuals.

It is possible for many a puppy's behavioral patterns to get stalled at this stage because he isn't allowed to act normally during the next two periods. This occurs especially among the toy breeds because of attitudes toward their size, but it can happen with any breed. When a puppy is not ever allowed to act like a dog (i.e., rough-and-tumble playing with other pups, investigating all corners of his world), never experiences stress of any kind, and has all his needs met before they even arise, he becomes a spoiled pet — a perpetual puppy. The breeder is cheating the dog by not allowing him to develop into a mature canid, and the owner is cheating himself of the pleasure of having a mature dog as a companion.

The Period of Curiosity
(Second Stage of Socialization)

36-49 days 5-7 weeks	Key Puppy Behavior: Weaning begins Curious Little sense of fear Participates in group activities and sexual play Dominance order is beginning

This is an *extremely important* time in the puppy's life. It is the period when the pup is totally dependent on the environment that you provide for him to stimulate and develop his genetic qualities. In addition to needing a stimulating environment, the pup must receive attention from people. The kinds of experiences that a puppy has during this period have a very strong effect on how he will react emotionally to humans when he is an adult. If he has little contact with people, except for being fed, he's probably not going to find it easy to accept human attention when he's older.

This is another time of rapid growth and change. During this period, a puppy acquires full use of his eyes and ears, his legs become stronger and more coordinated, and his brain reaches a final stage of physical development. Further development now largely depends on the experiences encountered by the otherwise fully equipped puppy.

At the beginning of this period, the puppy still has little sense of fear and is quick to approach anything and anybody. But by the end of these two weeks, he begins to be more cautious in his approach, which is all a part of learning to discriminate among sights, sounds, and smells. Pups that don't go through these two

The center puppy is demonstrating a dominance posture.
Photo by Janet Yosay.

periods of learning (having been isolated or overprotected) tend
to become hyperactive adults. They have not learned how to sort
out sights, sounds, and smells during these weeks and to identify
the significant ones.

Sexual play is evident at this age. Mounting is quite common
among male puppies, and sometimes females mount other puppies.
This is a normal part of puppy play and is important in teaching
puppies what is normal sexual response as they mature. While
mature males tend generally to confine their mounting to females,
mounting to signify dominance over another male continues in
maturity. Females also sometimes mount other females as a demonstration of dominance.

Many behaviorists agree that socialization reaches a peak by the
forty-ninth day. From here on, human relationships, though still
very important, begin to have a decreasing effect on the socialization of the puppy. In other words, the amount of individual attention that a puppy has received by the forty-ninth day can never

be made up without a proportionately larger expenditure of time and effort.

The seventh week (forty-ninth day) is considered by many breeders to be the right age for a puppy to go to his new home. By then the pup has had sufficient time with his littermates for developing adequate dog behavioral patterns. His new owner can easily become the pack leader and can give the pup individual attention and a lot of environmental variety. It is still essential, however, that opportunities for socializing with other dogs be made available on a regular basis. This ensures that the balance is maintained in interactions with other people and with dogs in the community.

The Period of Behavioral Refinement (Third Stage of Socialization)

50-63 days	Key Puppy Behavior
7-9 weeks	7 weeks: Has total hearing and visual capacity Will investigate anything
	8 weeks: Fearful of sudden and loud sounds and movement Cautious of anything new in the environment

The period of behavioral refinement is characterized by progression from unfettered curiosity to a more nervous evaluation of the stimulus created by the pup's environment. This reaches its height around eight weeks of age and persists to about ten weeks of age.

This stage is an important milestone in a puppy's life. He reaches full visual and hearing capacity, and his brain is physically mature. This means that the brain is ready to perform its physical processes and the pup can start learning to respond to your wishes as long as the learning process is taking place in very small steps. However, this doesn't mean that he's ready to be treated as an adult dog. He is still emotionally very immature.

This age is sometimes termed the "fear period" because the pup is very susceptible to long-lasting effects if he receives a bad fright during this time. Dr. Michael Fox has observed that at five and six weeks, a puppy can be severely frightened and in a relatively short period of time bounce back to his normal happy self again. However, during the eighth week, if the pup receives a bad fright, it may take weeks for him to return to his normal behavior in the same frightening situation. He may even carry the fear all his life. A loud, rough person, a spanking, or an abnormally sharp noise are examples of frights that can cause such a reaction. Thus, shipping a puppy to a new home by air freight during the eighth week could have a lasting bad effect. But don't think that you have to go to the other extreme and be overly protective, keeping your pup in seclusion. Let him have normal experiences.

Puppies at this age also become hesitant about new and different objects and situations. During the preceding period (five to seven weeks), the puppy usually approached the unfamiliar fearlessly. Now, at eight weeks, the pup is noticeably more hesitant in his approach. He may go back again and again to the same area or object as though he doesn't trust his initial judgment.

An example of this caution is seen with retrievers — the five- to seven-week-old puppy will splash in shallow water or happily bounce into heavy grass, cattails, or whatever is in his path. But during his eighth week, this same pup will start to be suspicious of water, even a shallow pond, or a pile of rocks, and he seems to think that diving into a patch of weeds is unthinkable, at least without a lot of sniffing and investigating first. However, by the end of the ninth week, this very pup is returning to his previous crash-bang self.

This is all another normal and important part of the socializing process, a continuation of sorting out the multitude of smells, sounds, and sights to determine what is important.

The Period of Environmental Awareness
(Fourth Stage of Socialization)

64-84 days	Key Puppy Behavior:
9-12 weeks	Develops strong dominant and subordinate behavior among littermates
	Begins to learn right behavior for right time
	Continues to improve in motor skills
	Has very short attention span

Even though no new behavioral patterns are evident during these weeks, the pup is beginning to learn the right behaviors for the right times. This is no small task, and it is a necessary stage for the pup to go through in the maturing process. His brain is ready for full functioning, but information must be fed into it one step at a time. It takes a puppy a long time to learn the acceptable ways of the world. This age is the culmination of the socialization process. Exposure to different environments (as discussed in Chapter 6) is the primary consideration here.

Up to this age, the puppy has been very self-oriented. Most of his learning has been "me"-directed. He has learned to like his new family. He knows where his bed is, where the food is kept, where there's a warm place for a nap, and (very importantly) where the urinating and defecating areas are. Now he's beginning to pay attention to *you*.

In fact, he thinks you're wonderful! He'll quickly learn his name. He'll come flying to you when you call him and get his attention. At this age, the puppy has a strong desire to please. After all, you're his whole world, having taken the place of mother and littermates.

The puppy pays attention to you, but he's also extremely busy learning everything he can about the world around him. The pup's brain tissue reached its full physiological growth around eight weeks of age, and now he's ready to learn, to have experiences that will teach him how to behave, how to act like a dog, how to

Developmental Periods of the First Three Months.

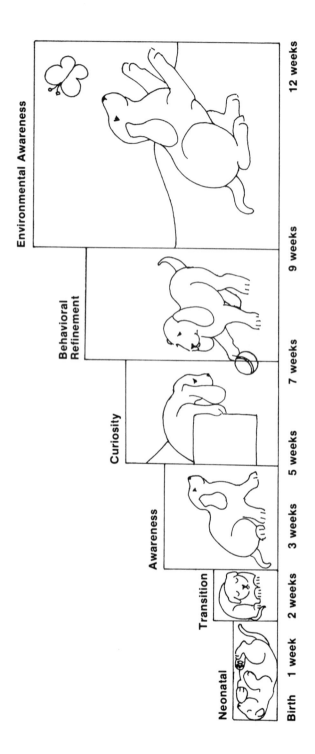

Neonatal | Transition | Awareness | Curiosity | Behavioral Refinement | Environmental Awareness

Birth   1 week   2 weeks   3 weeks   5 weeks   7 weeks   9 weeks   12 weeks

Table 3. Summary of Puppy Behavior—What You Can Expect

Age	Behavior
1 and 2 weeks	All activities are innate—only sucking, crying, crawling and touching. No sense of sight or sound. Is susceptible to cold temperatures. Must receive touching from bitch to stimulate elimination. Cannot learn anything at this age.
3 weeks	Eyesight and hearing dim but rapidly improving. Begins to walk briefly. Becomes interested in littermates. Able to start eating and drinking and to eliminate without the bitch's stimulus.
4 weeks	Needs a very stable environment. Becomes aware of multitude of sights and sounds. Learns that people are important. Should remain with bitch as much as possible.
5 weeks	Life becomes exciting! Not afraid of anything. Is very aware of people and likes to be with them.
6 weeks	Has full use of eyes and ears. Legs stronger and more coordinated. Investigates everything in sight.
7 weeks	Very involved with his own needs. Will seldom respond to name. (You must take initiative if you want him to follow you.) Can be started on housebreaking routine.
8 weeks	Occasionally responds to name. Hesitant about approaching new things. Needs to be able to take his own time about new experiences.
9 weeks	Will follow at your side for short distances. Likes to lie down beside or on top of your feet.
10-12 weeks	Almost always responds to name and comes when called from short distance. Will come running when he hears food pan rattle. Learns not to get stepped on. Becomes more dependable with housebreaking.

Photo by Margie Thayer.

please a human — quite a challenge for a pup, but one that he's ready for.

By ten weeks of age, strong dominant and subordinate behavior is displayed among littermates. In some cases, this behavior has been evident for three to four weeks. Any puppies remaining from the litter should start receiving individual attention and should receive their own special time alone with the breeder or other individual. Otherwise, the pups will begin bonding with each other, will lose their interest in people, and will become more difficult to train.

The last stage of socialization is a most delightful one. At the same time that you should be actively molding your puppy's behavior (he won't always be this small and eager to please), you should also be enjoying your puppy. Relax and have fun. A puppy stays little such a short time — he'll be grown up before you know it.

Photo by Cindy Noland.

This ideal bitch is calm and relaxed with her puppies.
Photo by Kent Dannon.

CHAPTER 4

THE BREEDER'S RESPONSIBILITY
(The First Seven Weeks)

A puppy's most important behavioral needs during his first seven weeks are a stimulating environment, exposure to mild stress, and individual attention.

Whether a litter is raised in the house or out in the kennel, whether the breed is a house dog or a sporting dog, there's much a breeder can do to encourage the development of emotionally healthy puppies.

Being a breeder of puppies is a very important job, one that should be undertaken with the commitment of the time and effort necessary to get the pups off to the best possible start.

Aside from a clean, warm home box area and adequate food, a young puppy has definite behavioral needs. During the first seven weeks, a puppy's three most important needs are a stimulating environment, exposure to mild stress, and individual attention. These needs can readily be met by the breeder if he or she recognizes them and then adjusts time schedules and the home environment to best satisfy the emotional growth requirements of the puppies.

Environmental Enrichment

The first two weeks of a puppy's life are in a separate world from the rest of his life. Even the instinctive behaviors that a puppy exhibits at this age aren't carried over into the "dog-behavior" world. Therefore, the breeder can't provide much enrichment during the first two weeks because the pup lives in his own silent, dark world. Environmental enrichment at this age consists of seeing that the mother is healthy and well fed and that the litter is in a warm, comfortable, clean area. During the puppy's third week, he's very engrossed in the mini-world of littermates and puppy-box area and consequently is not very receptive to environmental stimulations.

However, beginning with the fourth week (around twenty-two days of age), and from then on until seven weeks of age, the puppy is very busy learning to use his rapidly developing senses. You might ask if providing environmental stimulation is worth the bother for such a short period of time, from twenty-one to forty-nine days. Yes, it certainly is. We know from behavioral and physiological studies how rapidly the pup's nervous system is growing during these weeks. The breeder and the puppy's new master probably receive the greatest future rewards for the relatively small effort put forth during these days.

Three Through Seven Weeks

You don't need to dazzle the puppy with a clutter of items. Overstimulation certainly isn't the goal. Do your pups play in the backyard? The lawn furniture is an example of environmental stimulation. Moving the wheelbarrow around for cleanup is another example. This is what we mean when we say that a litter raised in a family home environment is automatically socialized and stimulated. However, when puppies are raised in a more iso-

Something as common as a lawn chair can provide environmental enrichment.

lated area of a pen or kennel, specific items need to be added to their environment.

Spending a lot of money isn't necessary. Use whatever is available to you. For example, set a couple of old wood stumps in the pen area. Cardboard boxes are marvelous and fall in the easy-come, easy-go category. These can be dens for a pup to go into or tunnels to walk through. One item that's very popular with one breeder's pups is a wood box about four feet long and two feet wide. It has two openings on diagonal ends of the long sides with carpet on the floor. The pup can go in one door and out the other or lie inside and look out, or run through, or whatever seems right at the time. Another good idea is short lengths of plastic or ceramic pipe — whichever size your pups can easily walk through. (Never take a chance with a pipe that might become too narrow as the puppies grow.)

One item that we consider almost essential for puppies is a platform of at least two steps, not too high for your five- to six-week-old puppy to navigate easily. The steps should have a large enough area on top so that the pup can feel comfortable before starting down again.

Use your imagination. Look around at garage sales and see what you can find. Safety is the primary concern. Sharp edges or material that can be easily shredded and possibly swallowed should not be used.

By four weeks of age, the puppy starts to leave the box or home base area to defecate and urinate. It can help the pup begin to learn the significance of carpeting if the sleeping box has carpet in it or if there is a narrow strip of carpet around the box so that his feet touch on the way out but he goes past it to tend to his chores. This gives him another texture to feel, as well as giving him the idea that carpeting is only for sleeping and sitting and walking.

Toys

Toys can add much variety to a puppy's environment. The first concern in selecting toys is safety; obviously, they should not be breakable or sharp. Toys that can be left with puppies in their play area are pieces of hard wood dowling cut to lengths that extend no more than one or two inches on either side of the puppy's mouth, and pieces of hard leather. From four weeks on, puppies like to mouth things and will use some of these items in "catch me if you can" games.

A wide range of chewing and play toys is available in pet-supply stores, but a puppy isn't interested in how much money you do or don't spend on toys. For a young pup, the important criterion is something he can pick up in his mouth or push and roll with his nose. Four-ounce cans (tomato sauce, for example) from the grocery shelf, with both ends smoothly removed, make enjoyable toys for some puppies that love to push them with their noses and make them roll, sometimes picking them up and carrying them briefly. Small cardboard frozen-juice containers are also excellent for this type of toy.

Puppies have preferences, and what attracts one may not interest another. A litter fortunate enough to live in a natural environment

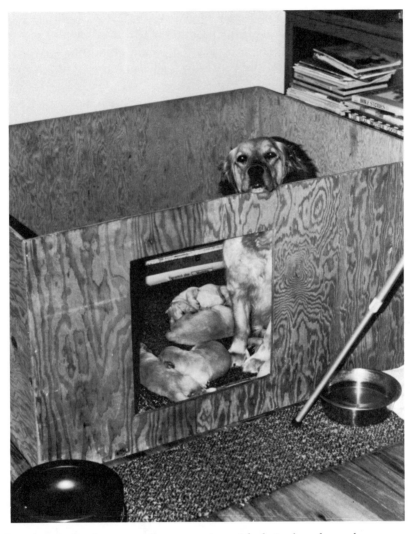

Puppies can begin to associate carpeting with their clean home box area which aids house-training.

will probably find all the toys it needs in pieces of twigs, leaves, pieces of bark, and the various items of nature that are about. Winter puppies or small breeds that are in a house or small kennel area need to have toys provided for them. The size of the pups would be a factor here. A toy has no value if it's too large, and it's dangerous if too small. A sturdy glove is a good toy; for example, a worn-out leather work glove is ideal. Think of the wealth of odors it has! A couple of knotted socks of different textures can be a lot of fun.

Old stuffed toys that have been rejected by previous owners can make good toys for some pups but obviously not for the type that will immediately rip them apart. The use of this toy will depend on your breed and on your particular pups. Button eyes should be taken out.

Feel free to experiment with household rejects that might make good toys for *your* pup. A puppy doesn't need a large number of toys as he grows up. A knotted sock to shake, a leather glove to carry around, and a couple of pieces of hard leather to chew are probably all the wealth he'll need from the age of four weeks on.

Exposure to Mild Stress

Even though the bitch is the primary influence in the puppy's life for the first twenty-one days, the breeder can already begin to influence a puppy's future behavior. Although the pup's eyes don't open until the end of the second week and his hearing isn't functioning until the third week, he will respond on a purely physical level to being touched. Touching and lifting the pup begins to condition his physiology to react at a very low level to changes in his experience.

Breeders who have made a practice of handling pups at a very young age have observed that these pups become very outgoing and confident as they get older. Fortunately, there is a study that verifies and expands this observation. Dr. Michael Fox, after conducting a study on the heart rates of puppies, concluded that mildly stressing puppies during the first five weeks will develop dogs that are superior when put in learning or competitive situations. Puppies that are handled at an early age and exposed to mild stress on a physiological level are better able to handle stress later in their lives without becoming emotionally disturbed or indulging in hyperactive behavior. As a result, they learn quickly and are more responsive to new experiences in different environments.

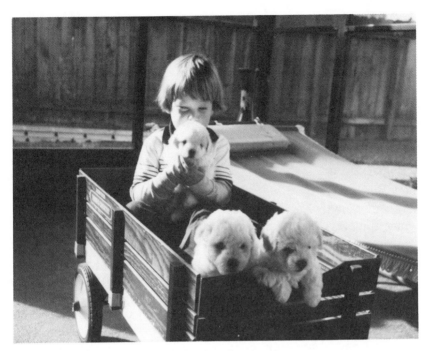

Puppies handled carefully by children learn to accept more stress.

Exposing puppies to stress is not another word for cruelty. We are referring to a *mild* stress. For the first two weeks, it involves picking up the pups on a regular basis. Many breeders automatically do this if they weigh the puppies regularly or if they just pick up each puppy each day to admire it. Putting the pup on the scale for weighing is an acceptable type of mild stress. However, a family with young children must very carefully supervise all contact with young children and must remember that too much handling can be worse than none at all.

During the first week, pick the puppy up each day. Rub his softness against your cheek, and admire his miniature perfection — these are the fringe benefits. Hold him for about a minute, with the puppy's body firmly supported with your hand under his tummy. Weigh him if you desire.

During the second week, seven to fourteen days, begin holding the pups in different positions briefly. On one day, turn the pup in a circle to the right, and on the next day, turn him to the left. The next day, hold him upright, followed the next day by holding him in a head-down position. On one day during this week, put the pup in a cold room for two minutes.

Occasionally, you will find a puppy that stiffens when picked up. This pup should be given the same routine as the others. If anything, he needs the brief but gentle stimulation to a greater degree than the others. But don't overdo it. More is not better. Pick him up gently once a day and then let him alone. This little guy will probably be a shy puppy, one that hesitates about everything and everybody in his environment. He will need to be placed in a quiet home and could make a fine companion for an older person. This pup should never be used in a breeding program no matter how beautiful he may be, and he or she should be neutered or spayed.

It also happens infrequently that a pup will show signs of brain damage, such as being able to move only in a tight circle. If you observe unusual behavior, consult your veterinarian about the severity of your particular case.

During the third week, fifteen to twenty-one days, the stress can be more specific. On one day, pick up the puppy and give a momentary pinch to his ear with your thumb and forefinger. Though he may cry out, he should calm very quickly. The next day, pick up the puppy and give him a momentary pinch between his front toes.

The fourth week, twenty-two to twenty-eight days, is a very stimulating one for the puppy. He is aware of all the many sights and sounds around him and is quite excitable. Because of this excitability, we feel that one stress event is sufficient for this week. About midway during the week, we like to take the pup from his littermates and put him on a different floor surface than he has experienced before. As well as being a stress activity for the puppy, this is also valuable for observation of the pup's behavior and probably doesn't take more than three to four minutes per puppy.

Put the puppy down on cement, wood, dirt or fine gravel, or linoleum if it isn't too slick for walking. If the area is bare, we will place a jacket on the floor, or put in a chair or anything that represents a different object for the pup to either approach or

Puppies learn bite inhibition through play. Note rickrack used for iden-
tification. *Photo by Kent Dannon.*

ignore. After you have put the pup down on the floor, begin to
record how he reacts to being alone, how quickly he begins to cry,
whether he walks around or stays in one place, or if he's investigating with his tail wagging.

The breeder can already begin to see differences in personality
in the litter, and it's interesting to keep a record of these. Make a
note of which pups are the most aggressive feeders and which ones
lose out in competition and seem to always end up on the outside
of the puppy pile. Which pups are the noisiest? Which squirm and
cry when picked up, and which settle down and enjoy it?

The most extreme behaviors stand out first, of course, but don't
forget to notice the pups that are in the middle range of temperament. These are the pups that likely will be easily trained as they
grow older.

If you have a large litter of all the same color, a dot of fingernail
polish in different areas on the puppies will help you to identify

them (right ear, left ear, middle of the head, each shoulder, the tail, etc.). You can also use a different color yarn for each puppy's neck.

During the fifth week, twenty-nine to thirty-five days, we give the pups mild auditory and visual stress. On one of the days, play a radio near the home box area when the pups are awake. Play it at a loud but not blaring level. If you have normal hearing and it sounds loud but not irritating to you, it will be sufficient. Five minutes is enough. This can be repeated again later in the day for another five minutes.

On another day of this week, give the puppy some mild visual stress. Four or five flashlights, manipulated by helpers, can be a sufficient number. Have the flashlights turned on and off for two to three minutes. Flicking the room lights will also suffice.

By the end of the fifth week, the mild stress activities become a minor factor, and the individual attention by the breeder takes over as the major aspect of the activities. Minor stress is still important and will continue to be a part of the individual attention, because there is a certain amount of stress every time the puppy is removed from his littermates and taken to a different place where he is expected to pay attention to you.

Individual Attention

Personal attention is important because it helps the puppy to develop a feeling of his importance as an individual. This, in turn, helps him to grow into a happy dog that is eager to please his owner. Your time alone with your puppy also helps him to learn that the name of the game is to be with people and to pay attention to people.

During the puppy's first three weeks, he isn't emotionally aware of the person who gives him individual attention, because his central nervous system hasn't reached that stage of development yet. The purpose during these weeks is to acquaint the puppy physically to the human touch and with a slight level of stress. From four weeks of age on, however, the puppy will be aware of you as a

A puppy needs personal attention to help him learn confidence in himself and in people.

person. Individual attention will help to imprint on the pup his place in the world of humans.

The fourth week is the beginning of the socialization period. There's no big mystery about socializing puppies; it consists of very simple, normal activities. It's just that the *socialization must be done.* The time is so short and goes so rapidly that often, even with the best of intentions on the part of the breeder and the new owner, pups don't get the variety of experiences that they need.

Puppies this age should have continuing human contact. A few minutes of individual attention for each pup during this week is important. We like to use our time for introducing each puppy to a new floor surface (discussed in the mild stress section). At least one other time this week, each puppy can be picked up, petted, and talked to.

By the fifth week, twenty-nine to thirty-five days, the central nervous system has developed very substantially, and the puppies now have sight, hearing, and smell (or scent), and are beginning to develop distance perception. However, even though the pups need the stimulation of people, sights, and sounds, emotionally they are still very immature, and they tire easily, so a little attention goes a long way. At least once during this week, but preferably twice, the breeder should take each puppy away from the puppy-pen area for at least ten minutes. The time can be spent with informal play. Bend down so that you can interact on your puppy's level and your face is close to him. Eye contact and facial expression offer a more intimate interaction.

This is a good age for *new* people and children to play with the puppies, provided caution is taken to see that the pups aren't overstimulated. In fact, if there are no children in the home, it's a good idea to invite a child to come and see the puppies. (The pups can have the needle-sharp points of their nails trimmed off.)

During the sixth week, thirty-six to forty-two days, it would be a catastrophe if you neglected to give each pup individual attention. It puts you in the category of being a producer, not a breeder, and you should never again have another litter in your care. (Yes, it's that important!)

The puppy's attitude toward people is noticeably changing now. When you took each puppy away from his littermates during the fourth week, the puppy was too young to be interested in any interaction with you. Even last week, the pup probably wasn't too interested in you personally, but now, at this age, most pups will run toward you and try to climb into your lap or jump on your legs. A two-way communication system is developing.

The process of building self-confidence and a good feeling about himself (yes, dogs need this, too) begins right now, at this young age. *A total of twenty minutes spent with each puppy away from the litter this week, preferably in two ten-minute sessions, is the best thing you can do to help that puppy begin to develop a well-adjusted personality.*

Occasionally, you'll have a puppy that will be very unhappy when removed from his littermates. This pup may act shy and be quite uncomfortable when taken to a different place. He may not want to come to you or may not even want to walk around and investigate the area by himself. When working with this puppy during his individual attention session, be sure that you are where the pup can neither see nor hear his littermates. Sit down on the floor or ground near the pup. Don't lean over him; that will only make him more fearful. Talk to him in a quiet voice. Pat your hand on the floor in front of him. Try to get his attention. See if you can coax him to come to you even if it's just a matter of his moving a few inches. This pup needs much gentleness. If you're an impatient person, don't try anything that will make you irritated when the pup doesn't respond the way you think he should. Just spend the time sitting close to the puppy. If neither of you moves for the first session or two, that's the way it is. The puppy will gradually become accustomed to your presence and will begin to approach you and investigate. This puppy will need to be placed in a family that is willing to work with this personality type, and he should be spayed or neutered. This type of puppy needs very special care. He will need to be placed in a family who understands that this puppy is socially handicapped and that he will require special care because of his sensitivity.

The individual session at the beginning of the seventh week should be about ten minutes long with each puppy. Call the puppy to you from a few feet away, walk closely in front of him, and coax him to follow. Sit down on his level with some gentle play. Stroke the pup. Talk to the pup, too. With your voice, try to get him to look at you.

By the end of this week, many puppies will be going to their new homes. The breeder can be confident that he or she has given the puppies every advantage possible in preparing them for their new life in their new packs.

Other Considerations for the Breeder

Weaning

If physiology and nutrition were our only concerns, the bitch could quickly become unnecessary to the pups because of the advancements of modern science. During the first few days, she has kept them warm and, because of her own vaccinations, she has given them passive immunity to infectious disease through anti-

Puppies first learn discipline from their mother. *Photo by Kent Dannon.*

bodies in her colostrum milk (the first milk after parturition). Beyond this point, milk mixtures are available that can replace the bitch's milk nutritionally. Theoretically, if this is all that weaning is, the pups could now be removed from the bitch. However, we think that weaning goes beyond the purely nutritional aspects and that it is a developmental process affecting the dog's future social adjustment.

The interaction of the puppies with the bitch and with littermates is profoundly important for at least the first five weeks. If you want a puppy that is well adjusted to his identity as a canid, then his relationships with other dogs are very important. For example, the puppy learns from his littermates or his mother just how much of a bite is too much. He learns through this experience that he must control the use of his jaws.

Puppies begin to eat supplemental food. *Photo by Deloris Reinke.*

As the pup approaches the age of five weeks, the period of curiosity, he begins to explore and will leave his mother and his littermates at times. Among wild canids, other adult members of the pack would interact with the pup, but with the domestic dog, this is the point at which people begin to take over the role of the canine mother, virtually reliving history and in doing so reinforcing the domestication of the puppy into the human world. Weaning is part of that domestication.

A breeder shouldn't accept any one specific rule for the weaning of pups. Much depends on the size of the litter, the size of the pups, and the attitude and health of the bitch. If the bitch's attitude and health permit, we think it best to keep her with the pups for at least five weeks. Supplemental feeding can begin at three weeks of age, which is often beneficial to both bitch and pups.

Raising the Single Puppy

Raising the single puppy whose mother has been able to nurse and associate with him is not very much different from raising a whole litter. You are the sole controller of socialization, however, as we presume that there are no other young dogs around. The more profound effects of not having littermates will be seen later — for instance, the early sexual play that occurs around six weeks is associated not only with sexual behavior but with dominance and submission. This type of dog-to-dog interaction, of course, cannot be simulated, so there is nothing that we can substitute. We believe that for this reason, and perhaps also because of deprivation of interactions between three and four weeks, the lone puppy may always have an awkwardness with other dogs in adult life. But this is not absolutely certain. If you find another young dog for yours to play with at least as early as twelve weeks of age onward, this may be adequate compensation.

The hand-reared pup that has neither mother nor littermates is a more serious matter. Dr. Michael Fox has noted that a puppy must recognize and be accepted by his own kind before he can relate well to a person. Many aspects of behavior can be learned only by interaction with the pup's own species, such as the social releasers of barking, tail-wagging, paw-raising, and genital-olfactory exploration. The hand-reared pup might appear "loveless" toward humans for this reason.

If you are raising a single puppy, you must handle your puppy a number of times a day — more than normal in the early weeks in order to avoid social deprivation — say four to six times a day for a total of at least twenty minutes. Lie down with him and allow him to bite and growl, threaten, bare his teeth, etc. You must interact like his missing littermates. Do not play roughly or violently. When puppy sinks his teeth too hard and hurts, push him away, growl and squeal, and then isolate him for several minutes. This way he learns the social limits of play, and this will be useful subsequently with other dogs and people. If you must punish, do it like the bitch — hold the scruff of the neck and shake a few times and growl to show displeasure. Demonstrate your dominance at such times by height, direct gaze, and a low growl. From eight to ten weeks on, carry on with the puppy training as for other puppies, but seek canine association as we have indicated.

You must control such association, as the other dog may not be an ideal companion for yours.

Shipping

Federal regulations state that a puppy may not be shipped by air until he is at least eight weeks old. However, even this isn't a good time, because the pup has a fairly high level of anxiety between eight and ten weeks of age.

Quite naturally, new owners want to get their puppy expeditiously, and breeders want their pups to get settled in their new homes as soon as possible. Remember that at this age the pup is very nervous. Since this is the period of behavioral refinement in which severe frights and trauma are to be avoided, it's best to wait until the pup is ten weeks old. He will be able to handle the stress much better. This allows time to condition the puppy to feel comfortable in his shipping crate.

Shipping stress can lead to physical sickness or, at this age, permanent emotional disturbance, putting the eight- to ten-week-old puppy in double jeopardy. The stress of travel can lead to a suppression of immunity to disease in a puppy or a dog of any age, which may increase the animal's chances of contracting an infection. This is something that you must discuss in detail with your veterinarian. We are more concerned right now, however, in trying to dissuade people from relinquishing puppies to a carrier with no control or knowledge of the emotional trauma that the animals might suffer en route. Often, the effects of the emotional stress of travel aren't recognized as being related to the trip, because it can take from two to four days for the problem to surface.

The breed and basic personality of the pup are factors in how the trip affects him. For a pup that has a tendency to be just a little shy, that is not vigorously outgoing, an air-freight trip could be devastating.

The shipping kennel should be sturdy with sufficient air movement, and not so large that the pup will be tossed around. Most airlines have adequate kennels for sale. Never ship a dog in a wire kennel unless it is covered with heavy canvas. The puppy needs to feel the relative security of the burrowed den, and if he is openly exposed to all of the sights and sounds of a freight depot, he could be seriously upset. Leaving the home den is stressful enough without adding to it unnecessarily.

If shipping is necessary, consult with your veterinarian about the requirements for a health certificate and steps that you may take to minimize stress and motion sickness.

Transporting by car. Many pups will settle down and ride in a lap nicely. If the pup is really excited, shake him vigorously (but not harshly) by the scruff of the neck, then put him on your lap or on the seat beside you.

If you're driving alone, the puppy might settle down beside you and not be a problem, but be prepared with a covered box or puppy kennel. Put it on the seat beside you and talk to the pup. If a puppy is suddenly removed from his littermates and dumped on the floor of the rear compartment of the car, his resultant fear may affect his emotional development. Furthermore, if he has motion sickness as well, this will make matters worse.

Don't Be Tempted to Keep Two

"If one pup is cute, two are cuter, and besides, they'll keep each other company." Wrong! If you raise two littermates, you're asking for disappointment. To oversimplify, the two pups will form a tight relationship and tune you out. You will never get the response or loyalty from either one that you should. If you're thinking of showing your dog or going into one of the dog sports, neither pup will form the intense communication with you that is necessary for top performance.

There is another reason for not raising littermates together. The more dominant puppy will become consistently more assertive and may develop the personality of a bully at the expense of a more submissive puppy that will begin to accept a consistently subordinate attitude as the accepted pattern of behavior. This would be a great disadvantage if the pup were expected to go into competition of any kind when older. It's best to leave the raising of littermates to a professional breeder or trainer who has the facilities and time to do a proper job of it.

A similar situation occurs when a pup is raised to maturity with the mother dog. The puppy is not likely to develop the same confident personality as when raised alone or with an unrelated dog.

Interestingly, the Guide Dogs for the Blind organization has never had a pup that had been raised with its mother or littermate become a guide dog. Again, it is possible to live happily with a mother-pup pair, but it takes a lot of extra time and effort on the part of the owner in separating them during puppyhood and in providing adequate dog accommodations to facilitate this.

Summary: Suggestions for Breeders

There are far too many litters of puppies produced without adequate thought given to the need for socialization and proper handling. If you plan to breed, you can make it a pleasant experience for yourself and ensure that the puppies you raise will be well-adjusted, happy pets by planning for the socialization and development in advance. Here are a few things to think about:

1. Don't plan a litter unless you are willing to provide the time and facilities necessary for proper socialization and care.
2. Select breeding stock with sound, well-adjusted personalities from a line of dogs with good temperament.
3. Cull from your breeding program any dogs that produce poor temperament such as shyness, aggression, or nervousness in their puppies. Also cull any dogs that exhibit bad behavioral traits that puppies may learn from association.
4. Spend at least five minutes every other day handling *each* puppy during the critical stage of five to seven weeks.
5. Provide stimulating facilities and toys for the litter. Introduce each puppy to a variety of environments before it leaves for its new home.
6. Avoid placing puppies in new homes during the critical eighth week if at all possible.
7. Educate your puppy buyers in the proper socialization, training, and handling of the puppy, and try to assure yourself that the buyer is interested enough to put in the time for this training and socialization before you sign the sales contract.
8. Follow up with your puppy buyers, and help them resolve behavioral problems at the onset.
9. Follow up on your puppies to make sure that personality problems are now showing up in the pups at an older age.

Children must understand the importance of holding a puppy correctly.

CHAPTER 5

PUPPY GOES TO A NEW HOME

"Enjoy getting acquainted with your dog, but don't expect
too much too soon."

Nothing equals the excitement of anticipating a new puppy! The fun of bringing a pup home and introducing him to his new family is a very special experience. What hopes we have for our perfect puppy! He will, of course, become a well-mannered dog, staying quietly at our side, eager to follow our every command. Well, it's a long road from the cuddly puppy to the mature dog, but with some effort and understanding, it can be traveled successfully. It all begins with Day One in the new home.

The first few days a puppy is in his new home can be trying for both the puppy and the new owner, because both are trying to adjust to a new situation. After all, the puppy finds that he has been suddenly taken from his den and littermates and is expected to immediately accept a new, foreign way of life. However, with patience and a sense of humor on the part of the new owner, the first few days can be accomplished with good feelings on both sides.

Breeders and behaviorists generally agree that seven weeks of age (forty-nine days) is the ideal age for a puppy to go to his new home, with seven to ten weeks being the most desirable age range. In families where there are preschoolers, we recommend that a pup not be introduced into the home during the eighth week.

The seven- to ten-week-old puppy still needs a lot of rest and will take morning and afternoon naps. For the first day or two, however, he might be very excited and spend much of the day in motion, checking out his new home. As long as he isn't hurting himself or anything else in the environment, let him investigate wherever and whatever takes his fancy.

Children should not be allowed to overtire the puppy.
Photo by Jan Whitaker.

If the puppy is eight weeks old when he first comes home, be very patient with him. This is the fear period, and sharp noises or harsh treatment will leave him with fear that may take months to overcome. Let him take his time getting acquainted with everything, and don't take him to places where he will be subjected to loud and frightening sounds or activities. If at all possible, trips to the veterinarian should be arranged either before or after the eighth week.

If the puppy is ten to twelve weeks old when you first bring him home, he'll be more rambunctious, especially if he's one of the larger breeds, and he'll sleep considerably less during the day. However, he's at an age where you can get his attention quite easily and where he'll want to please you and stay close to you. It's very important that the puppy's pre-training activities begin now.

The First Day

Before the puppy arrives at your home, we assume that you will have made adequate preparations, such as a bed with a blanket or a piece of carpet in it (a cardboard box works fine for this). Know where the puppy will be kept when you're absent from home during the day (backyard, kennel, or a puppy-proof room), know where you want the puppy to urinate and defecate, and have a supply of puppy food on hand and a food bowl and a water bowl. You will be much more relaxed if you have thought out these details before the puppy arrives.

The main concern with the first few days is in letting the pup get acquainted. Within the area where he is allowed to roam, give him lots of time on his own to sniff and explore, to find his bed area, to determine good nap-taking spots, and to learn where his food and water dishes are kept. Feed him a good-quality puppy food; the breeder of the pup will inform you what the puppy is currently eating. The seven- to eight-week-old pup is probably eating four times a day, which can be changed to three times a day, and around four to six months of age, to twice a day. We prefer scheduled mealtimes to free feeding because it helps with house-training. In addition, it shows your pup how reliable you are in the food department — same place, same time, same good food every day. As your pup grows, he'll gradually need to increase the amount of food, but don't let him turn into a butterball. Sometimes, because of an owner's work schedule, free feeding is the better solution. In this case, the main concern is that the pup doesn't overeat. Measure the amount of food put in the feed dish to keep a record of the quantity being eaten.

If the puppy is going to be kept in a pen area for a certain amount of time each day, be certain that he has a few toys available, and be certain that he won't be left for long periods of time. The ideal situation is for a puppy to be with someone a good bit of the time for the first week or two. The best time to initiate a puppy into your life, especially if the family is working or in school most of the day, is to arrange for the puppy's arrival during a period when someone will be home on vacation, at least for the first several days of the puppy's arrival.

The most difficult part of the puppy's first day is the first night in a new and strange place. This subject deserves a section of its own.

First Night Alone

The puppy's first night alone in his new home can be one of intense fear. The fear of suddenly being left alone can lead to anxiety that can show up later as a behavioral problem, such as excessive barking or digging at the carpet.

There aren't many alternatives for a pup's first night, and it is certain to be a stressful experience to some degree, but there is one method that works very well. Let the puppy spend his first couple of nights in the bedroom of his new master. Put a box in the room with a blanket or carpet in it, or just put the bedding on the floor beside your bed. The pup might ignore your efforts and select his own place, like under the bed or in a corner. Let the pup stay wherever he will relax and settle down.

A puppy is usually exhausted by nighttime and will sleep through the night. If not, a hand reaching down in the dark helps to calm him. (If this doesn't work, you'd better get up and take the pup out to urinate.) First thing in the morning, carry the pup outdoors

Keeping the puppy in the bedroom the first two nights makes the adjust-ment to a new home much easier for both the pup and the people.

or to the area covered with newspapers. You usually will have to carry him, because he might not be able to walk as far as that by himself without urinating until he's ten to twelve weeks old.

Two nights, or sometimes three, is usually enough of this special treatment. By then the pup should be ready to accept his bed in the regular place that you have selected for him. If you don't plan to allow the pup to continue sleeping in your room, it's best not to let him stay past the third night. If you wait much past that time, the pup will reach a point where he won't want to be moved, and you'll be back to where you started with the crying. If these special measures aren't possible, you had better buy some ear plugs and be prepared for loud crying for at least two nights.

You may want to consider allowing the puppy to continue sleep-ing in the bedroom. If you work and are away from home a lot, this is one way of giving your dog a sense of your presence and of your desire to be with him as much as possible.

Photo by Missy Green.

If you decide to do this, you should keep the pup in a crate during the night, or put the pup on a short rope tied to a leg of the bed until he's house-trained, with his own bedding there also, of course. The rope should be short enough to allow him to lie down without getting tangled.

Your Veterinarian

Your veterinarian is a vital member of the puppy-raising team. We believe that it makes good sense to select your veterinarian, and preferably get acquainted, before you even select the right puppy for you. Veterinarians deal with many breeds of dogs in sickness and in health and are only too happy to counsel you during that important time when you are making decisions about dog ownership and familiarizing yourself with the do's and don'ts.

Your veterinarian, if consulted early in your puppy's life, will be able to advise you of the things that you should be looking for and will make arrangements in advance for complete health counseling, checkups, and vaccinations.

If you have already acquired a puppy and have not yet consulted with a veterinarian, put this book down and do so right now. The veterinarian may not want you to go down there immediately, but he or she will make sure that a plan for a healthy and happy future for your puppy is worked out with you and subsequently implemented.

House-Training

Have you ever put a puppy outdoors, left him there for fifteen to twenty minutes, then let him in again only to have him immediately make a puddle or a pile on the carpet? It's very easy to believe that he's doing this on purpose, and it's very easy to get very angry. However, the pup simply doesn't have it all figured out yet. For one reason or another, he's still confused about the indoor-outdoor situation. Besides that, he doesn't urinate and defecate until he has the urge, and he didn't happen to get the urge until he was in on the carpet. It's going to take some time on your part to help him get the whole procedure straightened out. Some puppies learn in a few days, some not until they're three and four months old. Some puppies simply don't have the muscular control until they're several months old.

People tend to get very excited over the process of house-training. What's needed is a realistic philosophy — plus a lot of paper towels and carpet deodorant.

At what age can you expect your pup to be reliable in the house? The answer is as variable as the puppies to whom it applies. In puppy classes, we have owners who say that their pup had only two accidents and has been trained ever since. Other owners say that their pup is four months old and sometimes still has an accident. Some pups adapt to a routine very quickly, and some people adapt to being consistent in training. Some pups have stronger muscle and bladder control than others. There are many factors that affect the age at which your pup will be reliably trained.

As explained in the discipline section, spanking does more harm than good, and this is especially true in house-training. Many puppies react negatively to spanking. This can create additional problems and often actually prolong the training procedure. The least painful approach for both the owner and the pup is to establish a routine and to praise the puppy for performance at the proper time in the proper place. Follow these guidelines:

- Feed the pup at the same times every day, and when he's finished eating, immediately take him outdoors. Take the puppy out immediately after he awakens from a nap and after a play period, or even in the middle of a play period if it's a long and vigorous one.
- Keep your pup in the same room with you where you can watch him. If necessary, tether him to you by tying a long line around your waist so that the pup can't get more than three or four feet away from you.
- When you can't keep an eye on him in the house, put him outdoors or keep him in his crate — not longer than two hours for eight- to ten-week-old puppies, and not longer than three to four hours for older pups. Every time he comes out of his crate, take him outdoors immediately.
- If you are gone during the day and the pup is kept in the house, confine him to a room that's easy to clean and that can be mostly covered with newspapers (or you can simply clean up the floor). Gradually decrease the space covered by paper to only one small area. When the pup is older, probably around three months of age, remove the paper and train him for outdoors only.
- Take the puppy to the same outdoor area each time, and stand around and wait. If he doesn't do anything, return to the house, leaving him outdoors for a while if possible. Watch him, then go out and praise him if he does anything. If he comes in without

doing his chores, take him back out every five or ten minutes until he has success.

- If you catch your pup in the act, don't spank, but tell him what you think and rush him outdoors.
- Clean up and deodorize the area with either a vinegar-water solution (one part vinegar to four parts water) or a commercial cleaner. Otherwise, when a puppy gets a whiff of that particular odor, an eliminative reflex is set off, and thereafter he does what is natural for him.
- For nighttime, remove the water dish a couple of hours before bedtime. Take him outdoors at bedtime, then put him either in a small, easily cleaned room or in his crate at your bedside. A pup can sleep several hours in a crate, and he will awaken you when he needs to go outdoors. Most pups adjust to their owners' sleep schedule reasonably quickly, depending on the age of the pup.
- Praise your pup every time he does his chores in an appropriate place. Praise shows the puppy what you want him to do and where.
- Use a key phrase, such as "hurry up." This will help in the future to cue your dog to get busy and stop daydreaming.

For the pup that is still not house-broken by four to four and a half months of age, get busy with your puppy training. Evaluate the relationship between you and your pup. Are you alpha? Does the pup respond to you when he hears his name? Does he come to you when you call from a short distance? Maybe your pup thinks that the house is his and that he can do whatever, wherever he wishes.

House-training is your responsibility. The pup is only doing what comes naturally.

Crates and Kennels

Another means of controlling the puppy so that he doesn't have accidents when you're not home is to train him to stay in a crate. As with everything else in puppy training, this is done gradually.

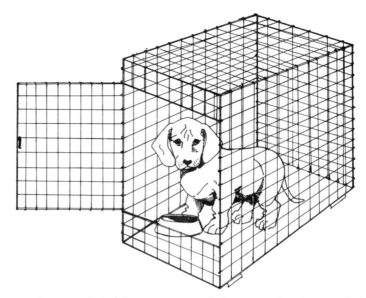

The crate is a very helpful way to control the puppy for short periods of time.

Have the crate always available, leaving the door open. Drop pieces of his food inside, and he'll quickly become very comfortable with going in to eat the pieces. Use it as his bed if possible. You can feed him in it. When you first close the door, stay there with him, talking to him. Open it after a few minutes and praise him, even if he did make a fuss. It will gradually become his "place" and he'll feel very secure in it.

The puppy shouldn't be confined continuously (except at night), but a crate can be a big help for an hour or two at a time. As the pup grows older, he can spend longer periods of time in a crate as long as it isn't a regular long-term arrangement. A crate is also excellent for car travel. It keeps the dog safe from sudden stops and swerves, and it keeps the people safe from an excitable dog.

There's nothing cruel about using a crate. It's very natural for a dog, because it fits into his den concept. Most dogs that have their own crates consider them a place of security. The only conceivable problems arise if the pup is forced into the cage suddenly and becomes frightened, or if he is left in it for hours at a time and becomes excessively lonely and bored.

Some families find a backyard kennel or pen area a necessity for confining the dog to a particular area of the yard. This offers protection for flowers and landscaping during the puppy's rambunctious growing-up months or when the puppy is left outdoors with no people present. These can be made of chain link and can be an attractive area, easy to keep clean.

Care must be taken, however, not to put the puppy in his kennel and then forget about him. Everyone in the twentieth century is busy, but if you're too busy to have the puppy out of the kennel everyday to be with you in the house or in the yard, then you're too busy to have a dog. Yard kennels are a convenience if used properly but should never be considered for twenty-four-hour-a-day confinement.

A pen keeps the pup from destroying plants in the yard but the puppy should be trained and played with every day.

Play

Play is an important part of the maturation process. A puppy learns what his abilities are by playing — play sharpens the senses of sight and scent. Play also stimulates the brain, keeping the pup alert and interested in his environment.

Play can be as simple as a running game — inviting the pup by giving the canine signal for play (a play-bow, putting your hands on your knees and bending over). Take a quick step, and the pup will probably start running around you in a circle. After the pup learns his name, you can play hide-and-seek — hide when you call him to come to you. Run up the stairs or to the next room, or behind a door. Keep calling until he finds you and discovers how happy you are to see him. Another running game is the round-robin. Position family members or friends around the yard. Take turns calling the pup, and have each person praise the puppy enthusiastically before the next person calls.

Puppies can make a game out of an old rag. *Photo by Deloris Reinke.*

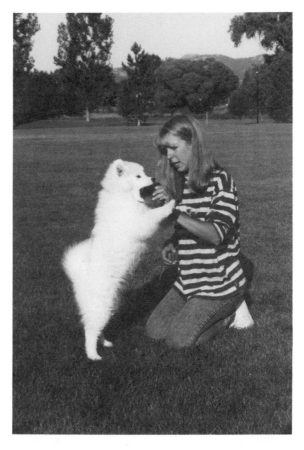

Balls are great toys and provide opportunities for interaction with your pup. *Photo by Joyce Woolley.*

A variety of toys encourages play, and a toy box on the floor for storage keeps them from cluttering the house. A squeaky toy and a puppy is a delightful combination, with the pup pouncing, tossing, stalking, and seeing how much noise he can produce. Soft, stuffed toys made for dogs are marvelous fun, but if your pup will rip it apart, it can't be left in the toy box — just get it out for short periods of time when you can watch. Put a knotted sock in the toy box for this pup. One pup had a teddy bear for his favorite toy, and he never chewed it — he just carried it around — and it was still a favorite two years later. This, however, is an exception. Balls are great toys. To begin, just sit on the floor with your legs out and roll the ball. When your pup has it, pat the floor to

Don't leave slippers out unless you want them used as chew toys.
Photo by Elaine Wishnow.

encourage the pup to run back to you. With the older pup, bounce
the ball and have the pup learn to catch it in the air. Balls designed
to roll in crazy directions are a delight for many puppies. Retrieving
is a good game for exercising your pup. See page 78 for suggestions
to teach this.

Chew toys serve multiple purposes — pups love something hard
to vent their chewing desire, and this also starts to wear off the
sharpest points of their baby teeth. Sterilized bones, nyla bones,
and rawhide pieces serve this purpose. Use rawhide sparingly if
your pup tears it apart too quickly and swallows the pieces. Shoes,
socks, magazines, purses, baseballs, and mitts are also some of a
pup's most favorite toys. If you don't want your puppy chewing
these items, however, keep them out of reach.

Play hide-and-seek with your pup's toys. Put a toy behind a
piece of furniture. "Where's the squeaky? Find it!" Help him to

find it until he learns the game. Use the name of his favorite toys often. Pretty soon, he'll learn which toy to go get from his toy box when you call it by name.

Tug toys are a very popular item in pet stores and can be used either to good advantage or, with some pups, not used at all. For independent pups that don't have much interest in playing with you, a tug-of-war game allows you and your pup to interact with each other and to develop your own version of the game. For other pups, tug-of-war games encourage aggressiveness or excessive mouthiness. These pups obviously shouldn't play this type of game. A rule of thumb to determine how much of this characteristic is in your puppy is to note his tendency to get too excited and your inability to halt the game. If the pup won't stop, tears your shirt sleeve, grabs at your hand, and loses control of his bite inhibition, this game isn't for him.

Most puppies will readily play with other dogs and puppies, as well as by themselves with a favorite toy, but the play that we truly want to encourage is a one-on-one activity. It's worth the effort, because there's nothing sadder than a grown dog that doesn't know how to have fun with his people.

Puppies and Older Dogs

Young puppies should never be left alone with older dogs unless you *know* beyond a doubt how the older dog treats rambunctious youngsters. There's a good reason for this. Some puppies don't begin to show submissiveness until they're about four months of age. Until they reach that point, they don't have an ounce of sense around older dogs and will usually pester them until the dog puts a stop to it. This might be done in a manner that doesn't injure a dog, such as scruff-shaking or snapping and growling. However, it might also be done with a bite that can injure a small puppy seriously. Don't take that chance.

By the time the puppy is four months old, the risk of injury becomes much less. The pup begins to assume the submissive posture of rolling on his side when threatened by an older dog, and this acts as a damper on the situation. A puppy at least four months old knows enough to move out of the way quickly, too.

Photo by Diane E. Brown.

CHAPTER 6

SOCIALIZATION CONTINUES
(Eight to Twelve Weeks of Age)

A puppy's two most important needs during the eighth to twelfth weeks are: exposure to a variety of environments and building of self-confidence.

An EEG normally shows adult brain waves in an eight-week-old puppy. This tells us that whatever activity a puppy participates in is being recorded by the central nervous system and is going into the puppy's data bank. This is why we say that the manner in which you treat your puppy now will have an effect on his future behavior.

By this age, many puppies have arrived at their new homes. If a puppy stays with the breeder beyond eight weeks of age, it will be a time-consuming process for the breeder because each puppy *must* be given a great deal of individual attention and exposure to different environments.

If you're a potential new owner and are considering buying an older puppy, be certain to acquire the puppy from a conscientious breeder who has taken the time to continue the socialization process beyond the first seven weeks. Puppies that are ignored and left in a kennel to grow until their show quality can be determined, or that are just the last to be sold, are prime candidates for being kennel shy. These pups past twelve weeks of age find it very difficult to form a strong attachment to a person and are more difficult to train because of their shyness (which is basically a result of a lack of self-confidence). However, if a pup has been given sufficient individual time and a variety of experiences, he can become a good addition to the family even when acquired past the age of twelve weeks.

The same conditions apply when a puppy is brought to his new home during the ideal age of seven to ten weeks. If this pup is stashed away in a pen and ignored, except for feeding and an occasional romp around the yard, until he's "old enough to learn something," he'll also have kennel-shy symptoms and will be much more difficult to train and to form a close attachment with when older.

Variety of Environment

Giving your pup different experiences is important to personality development even if he's going to be a house dog that seldom leaves home. His experiences give him a basis of confidence on which to build a mature personality. If the pup knows only the backyard, he needs to take a walk out front, in a field, in a school yard on Sundays, or to a friend's or neighbor's home. A variety of different areas close to home will be satisfactory. *It's important to remember that the pup goes through a fearful stage at eight weeks of age, and so he should not be taken to any place of loud noises and confusion during that week.*

If there's any possibility that you might show your dog, enter obedience trials, or participate in sled-racing or one of the various

Puppies that are allowed to freely investigate their environment learn to handle their fears.   *Photo by Deloris Reinke.*

types of field trials, this environmental stage of the puppy's development is *vitally* important. Without a variety of experiences at this stage, the pup may not gain the basic attitude necessary to perform adequately in unfamiliar areas away from home. If he isn't introduced to different areas, he may end up being a backyard genius —perfectly brilliant at home but not worth a nickel anyplace else.

Ideally, a puppy should be exposed to at least three different environments during these weeks. If the area is such that the puppy can be off the leash, that's great. At this age, he'll probably not wander too far away from you, but if his nose begins to carry him on and on, get his attention and call him back to you by clapping your hands, turning and running, or bending down on your knee. Even though most of the time is spent free-running, this time can also be used for a short session of leash training. Long visits aren't necessary. Fifteen to twenty minutes are sufficient for each visit to a new place.

This puppy should be on leash to prevent possible injury.
Photo by Korrey Tweed.

If the area that you're in requires the pup to be on leash, this will mean that the puppy will become leash-trained out of necessity. Let him have as much freedom as possible on the leash, and don't demand that he walk at your side the whole time. This will help him to grow up as a socially confident dog. In addition, a puppy of this age needs exercise for all of that energy.

Taking the pup for walks in different places is a good way of helping him learn to accept new experiences and to trust what his senses tell him. This will help him to adjust to being a dog in a man's world.

Building Self-Confidence

The more confidence a pup has, the more quickly he learns. It's easy to build confidence. Talk to your pup. Tell him how good he is (when he is good). Keep him with you as much as possible. You don't have to fuss with him or play with him all of the time. In fact, it's best not to, but it's extremely important that he not be isolated for long periods of time, that he can sit on your feet while you're peeling potatoes or lie beside your chair when you're reading the paper. Then if he wanders about the room and gets into mischief, you'll be able to correct him on the spot so that he'll be learning how to please you as well as what does not please you. This learning how to act around people is all part of acquiring a feeling of self-confidence.

Some people say that their pup is too wild to be allowed in the house, but this is often a result of the vicious circle. The pup is wild in the house because he's so excited. If he is allowed to be in the house most of the time that you're home, and if you keep an eye on him to distract him from mischievous activities, he'll soon learn how to behave nicely.

An excellent means of building self-confidence in a puppy is to spend time alone with him, playing with him, grooming him, and beginning to teach him behaviors that are important to you, such as to sit, to come, and to walk along beside you.

Grooming

Brushing can certainly be included in the puppy's routine by this time. Begin very gradually. Thirty seconds is long enough to have the puppy standing (relatively still) while you brush him. Praise him just when you are able to accomplish a couple of brush strokes as well as at the end of the grooming session. This is very important, because the puppy must know when he has pleased you. Gradually increase the length of time you work with the pup. You'll notice a slow, steady improvement in the cooperation of the puppy. If you've timed your praise well, the pup will realize that grooming is a pleasant experience to be shared with you even though tangles might occasionally complicate the situation.

While you work with your pup, tell him how handsome he is and how well he's behaving. Building his confidence is very important, whether he's going to become a show dog, an obedience or field dog, or an important member of the family.

If you're wishy-washy in your attitude toward grooming and toward having the pup stand still for a few seconds, your pup will

Teaching the young puppy to stand will help with combing and brushing.

sense this. He will take advantage of you and never stand still. In this case, you'd better read the chapter on molding behavior. You might have to give the pup a scruff-shaking to make him realize that you're the boss.

Introducing the Puppy to Pre-Training Activities

Building self-confidence and teaching a pup to do different things is a round-robin situation. The more confidence a puppy has, the better he learns. By the same token, when a puppy is learning to do new things, he is also gaining more confidence in himself and in his abilities.

This type of puppy activity is not a rigid training session. We're working with emotionally immature animals susceptible to fears and to confidence-destroying tactics similar to those that affect the human child. This is why "training" is not the best word to use. The term "pre-training" better indicates the intent of these activities — assuming that such a term does not belittle their importance. We assure you, work at this age will pay big dividends in the learning attitude of your dog when he is older.

The Collar

Puppies should become comfortable wearing a buckle collar at eight weeks of age. Continually check the collar for tightness, because pups often grow in spurts and a collar can become too tight in a very short time. Do not use choke-chain collars with puppies.

The Leash

Puppies also need to learn about leashes, which should be as lightweight as possible. We periodically see a young pup sporting a stiff, thick, heavy leash with a thick, heavy clasp. These are often bought in supermarkets and are much too heavy and stiff for puppy training.

Leash Training

Clip the leash to the collar, and when the puppy starts walking, go his way. Follow along for a few minutes, then release the pup from the leash. Another suggestion: some pups get very excitable on the leash, so when the pup is in the yard and ready to go back into the house, put the leash on him while he's trotting in happily. He'll be intent on returning to his home area and shouldn't be bothered by the leash. Then there's the pup that insists on chewing the leash. Encourage him to pay attention to you by coaxing with your voice and patting your leg as you walk. Keep the puppy moving at a brisk pace, almost a run, and you should be able to keep his attention on you rather than on the leash.

The Sit

Pups are never too young to begin doing sits. Anytime you have a couple of minutes and the pup is there with you, do two or three sits in succession. You don't need a leash on the pup for this. One method is the jackknife procedure. One hand will be on the pup's

Keep calling your pup, even when he gets distracted. *Photo by Jane Exon.*

chest, the other under his tail behind his knees. Call his name and say "sit" while you jackknife the pup into a sitting position. To do this, push back on his chest and forward on the rear of the stifle joint (behind the knees). The puppy is wiggling, so practice your coordination and do it quickly. Praise him immediately. Don't make the puppy stay in a sitting position. That comes later.

The other method of teaching the sit is discussed in the training chapter. Hold a tidbit right on top of the pup's nose, and move it back parallel to the floor. The pup will sit as his head moves back to follow the tidbit. Praise him as soon as he sits.

The Come

Begin teaching the come from seven weeks onward, and teach it anytime and any place around the house or yard. You do not need to have a leash on your puppy for this. The young puppy loves to come running and lick you in the face. You're his whole world. Take advantage of this, especially with the shy and the independent puppy that might initially resist coming to you. Get the pup excited while you are standing right in front of him, then run backward several feet. Give lots of happy praise and a tidbit — even independent pups usually can't resist a piece of hot dog or liver. If you have a busy pup that is distracted easily, begin the come at very short distances — maybe three to four feet. Begin as close as necessary to get the pup's attention and to achieve success. Gradually lengthen the distance. What's important at this stage is the pup's attitude — he *wants* to come running to you because it's such fun!

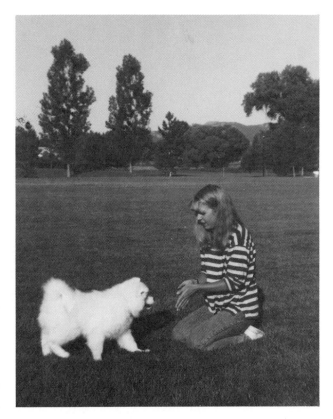

Begin teaching the "Come" as close as necessary to get the pup's attention. *Photo by Joyce Woolley.*

Retrieving

Retrieving is a great game to teach your puppy, even if your pup isn't a retriever. Ten to twelve weeks of age is an ideal time to start this. It's not only an easy and pleasant way to exercise a dog, but is also the basis for many other tasks that the dog can learn in the future, such as carrying the newspaper. (Another excellent way of giving a dog self-confidence is training him to do things for you.)

First, let your pup have fun with the chase. Tie a white sock or rag to a string, and wiggle it in front of the pup. When he shows interest, pull it along the floor and let the pup chase it. Pull it around you on the floor in a wide circle, just ahead of your pup. Then slow down so that he can catch it, or bring it in toward you so that when he pounces on it, he's close to you and you can praise him before you take it from him.

Now use a ball. Roll it to a wall so that the ball will roll back toward the pup. Coax the pup to you and praise him vigorously. Put a cord or a leash on the puppy so that when he decides not to bring you the ball, you have a handle to stop him from running farther away while you coax him to bring you the ball.

Important Basic Information for Teaching Puppies

Here are some basic guidelines that you can adopt as you work with your puppy to teach him good house manners.

Don't Get Tough

Emotionally and psychologically, the pup is still extremely sensitive. This means that learning takes place quickly, but that fears can also occur easily and thus inhibit learning. Pups cannot take pressure or harsh treatment. Repetition is the key.

Keep It Simple

A pup learns to do things in a step-by-step manner. If you expect a pup to do something before you've properly taught him to do it, the pup will lose his confidence and will learn not to try. The same pup, given a simple, step-by-step training approach, will become a dog that is eager to learn and that is ready for more complicated training as he gets older.

Be Brief

Puppies have a very short attention span. A pup learns only while he's paying attention to you, and you won't accomplish anything if you keep on training when the pup is mentally tired, even though physically he may still be very lively.

Build Confidence

Relax while you're with the puppy, smile, speak in a pleasant voice, and play running games with him. It's important at this age for the pup to feel that he's a valuable individual. Do your training exercises in a relatively quiet place. Because he's so playful, the pup is easily distracted by other people and activities. If he's constantly being interrupted by other sights and sounds, it will be difficult for him to get the message that you enjoy being with him and think that he's wonderful.

Use Words

Don't expect your pup to be a mind reader. The only way that he'll learn to associate the command with the action is if you use the word every time you guide him into doing what you want. A puppy can learn a very large vocabulary with such words as "outdoors," "bedtime," and "go for a walk," as well as the common commands.

Don't Expect Overnight Results

Try to stay relaxed as you work with the pup. Puppies learn in spurts and starts. One day, he may know absolutely everything and perform to perfection. The next day, it's as though he never had a moment's training. Too many trainers make the mistake of thinking that if their puppy does it right once or twice, he knows it forever. But it really takes hundreds of repetitions for a puppy to learn something. He may go through several periods of confusion in the process. You may think that he's mad at you or is trying to spite you. In reality, he's probably trying to tell you that he's confused for some reason. This is often caused by some unknown factor. Perhaps you've done something a little differently, or the environment has changed in some way and his confidence has been shaken. Try to determine the cause of the behavioral change, then continue your training program. It will all iron out with time and effort.

If you take these suggestions into consideration, you are automatically teaching your pup to pay attention. By adhering to his physical and psychological needs, you'll find that he will respond to you and you'll be well on your way to building a good puppy-person relationship.

Photo by Jane Exon.

CHAPTER 7

DOMESTICATING YOUR PUPPY:
Shaping Your Pup's Behavior

Barring extremes of shyness or aggressiveness, there is enough potential variation of behavioral patterns that you'll be able to modify your puppy's behavior to fit in with your life-style. You do this by encouraging the characteristics that you like.

Much of a puppy's future behavior is set by what he experiences between three and fourteen weeks of age. His basic attitude toward people and his desire to please are established during these weeks. This chapter discusses the many possibilities that new owners will have to mold the behavior of the pup to fit into their life-style. This is the age when the owner and the pup's environment are both having a very strong influence in the development of the puppy's mature personality. Hard work during this period pays big dividends the rest of the dog's life.

Begin Now

It comes as a surprise to many people that their puppy is already developing behavior habits from the day he enters his new home. An example of this is how a puppy can learn to sit for his food dish before he even knows the sit command.

Hold the food dish up, back and over his head. The instant the pup's rear moves in a sitting direction, get the dish to the floor. The first few times you try this, the pup may not look like he's going to sit. Try to time the food dish delivery with a bending of his hind legs. After several days of good timing on your part, the pup will be sitting when he sees you with the food dish. This is an example of how easily a pup's behavior can be molded, beginning as early as seven weeks of age.

A pup can just as easily be conditioned to bite your pant leg or to bark at you. If your response is to pick him up and hold him in an effort to stop the behavior, the pup perceives this as a reward (even though unintentional on your part) and therefore sees the behavior as acceptable.

A puppy's behavior is constantly being molded all day long in this same manner. Whenever we praise the pup, or pat or cuddle him, the behavior immediately preceding is being *encouraged*. Whenever we speak sharply or distract the pup or discipline him, that behavior is being *discouraged*. Puppies develop habits very quickly. If you can control *your* behavior and pay attention to what actions you're rewarding, you're going to end up with a nice dog that you'll be happy to have around the house. It's much easier to encourage good behavior than to change bad behavior after the puppy has been allowed to get away with it.

The Bonding Process

Bonding occurs most readily between the age of seven to sixteen weeks. To ensure that a pup will be responsive to his owner as well as to other people throughout the rest of his life, he needs to bond to someone at this age. In a puppy's perspective, bonding means that he has someone to respect, to trust, to play with, and to show him what he can and cannot do. He has someone who cares. To you, bonding means that your pup will follow you around the house and look to you for approval of his just being there.

Bonding is the process of putting yourself first in your pup's priorities. It's your pup looking at *you* when you say his name; it's your pup coming to *you* when you call him, rather than running on past. To accomplish this bonding takes time spent one-on-one with your pup, taking walks with your pup, and not giving up if your pup doesn't respond as readily as you think he should. The independent, dominant, or overly busy puppy can reach a high degree of bonding if *you* keep working with him. So don't throw your hands up in impatience.

An excellent way to begin the bonding process is to tether your pup to you. Put your pup on a six-foot leash, and tie it around your waist or through a belt loop. The leash must be long enough for the pup to be able to sit or lie down, but you don't want a cord so long that it lets him wander several feet away from you. As you go about your business around the house, don't give your pup any commands such as sit or down. If he insists on jumping, give a quick, downward tug on the leash close to the collar. Prohibit biting or chewing by a swift bump or a sharp "no!" Tether your

Tethering can be done anywhere around the house.

pup at least twenty minutes (longer if possible) for several days. Your pup is beginning his one-on-one relationship with you. The more independent your pup's personality, the more he needs this process.

Because bonding is in process at this age, you need to give special attention to how you teach your pup about good house manners, and you need to learn what disciplines you should and shouldn't use.

Punishment

There's no place for punishment with young puppies. Hitting a puppy with a newspaper, or spanking with your hand is cruel punishment for *any* misbehavior. It certainly appears to be effective because your pup immediately stops his bad behavior and looks sorry for what he's done (unless he's dominant-aggressive, in which case he might challenge you), but puppies don't understand this punishment. It works against their natural attraction to people. It can build a wall of defense mechanisms that results in a dog that is more difficult to train and to communicate with when he's older. What you've gained in immediate release of your anger, you've lost in your dog's confidence and total trust.

Another abusive discipline is loud, angry, emotional shouting. A human voice with a nasty tone to it can put a touch of panic in your pup's mind, or if he's independent, stubborn or dominant, it can make him turn more into himself, becoming more and more unresponsive to you. Your pup is a baby. The purpose of this book is to help you get your baby dog off to a good start. Your attitude and approach to discipline is part of the bonding process and involves establishing yourself as the alpha member of your puppy's new pack. Puppies do need discipline at times — the right kind of discipline.

A major aspect of the bonding process involves establishing yourself as the alpha member of your puppy's new pack. Your role as pack leader begins when you bring the puppy home, and it is a matter, at this age, of your attitude and approach to discipline.

Discipline

Very few of us live with the perfect puppy. A busy puppy, full of joyful energy, can get himself in trouble because he doesn't know what he can and can't do around the house. We use discipline to correct a puppy's bad (from our point of view) behavior. When we correct a behavior, we are saying to the pup, "I want your attention right now. What you're doing is not okay." We want to halt that behavior, gain his full attention, then show him what behavior we do want from him. Fortunately, a variety of disciplines exist to effectively help the pup understand what behaviors we don't like. Praising our pup's good behavior helps him to understand what behaviors we do like.

Distraction

Distraction followed by praise works very well in molding your pup's behavior. Much of the mischief that a puppy gets into is a result of busyness. Many behaviors, like pulling on drapes or unrolling a roll of toilet paper by running through the house carrying the end of it, are not repeated once the pup has been distracted and gone on to other things.

If your pup is young — seven to ten weeks old — or is especially sound sensitive, use your voice to distract him. A loud "uh-uh" or a hand clap, or a slap on a table to startle the pup, will divert his attention to you. If the pup is ignoring you, use a shake can. For puppies, a Tums™ bottle with a few pennies in it makes an impressive sound to divert a pup's attention from his current mischief. The flat-sided bottle fits nicely into your pocket, making it handy and ready for action. For some pups, you might want to put the pennies in an empty pop can to make a louder distraction. When your pup is involved in a "no-no," shake the can. The startle effect should stop his action. When he looks up in surprise, distract him, talk to him, call him to you (you are very close), and praise him for being a good puppy.

Good behavior consists of simply not doing what he has been doing. If he's *not* doing whatever it was you didn't like, then he must be a good puppy — so tell him. How else will he know? Your praise is calm, not exciting. You are simply telling him that you prefer his good behavior over his bad behavior.

1. For the small pup the scruff shake is one hand on both the collar and scruff. A brisk shake lifts the front feet off the floor.

2. For the older and larger pup, the scruff shake is with both hands. Make eye contact as soon as shake is finished.

Canine-Type Discipline

To teach a puppy that he can't do "that" anymore, you have to catch him in the act and discipline him. How do adult canids discipline young canids? Primarily by using the element of surprise. When the pup is disciplined the first time — such as for trying to share a bone — the adult dog might snarl and grab for the pup, sometimes pinning him down. The pup is startled so abruptly that he often cries as though he's been mortally wounded. Following that initial discipline, it takes only a curl of the lip or a quiet growl to remind the pup of what not to touch, or where not to go. Of course, with some pups, particularly the very lively ones, the discipline wears off rather quickly, and then the pup asks for it again. He is startled into submission, and the cycle of good behavior begins once more.

We can use canine-type discipline to simulate the way adult dogs would discipline puppies. These can be very effective if done appropriately. Timing is the essence here, because the element of surprise is a major part of the effectiveness. The scruff-shake and the put-down are vigorous types of discipline, but there are milder disciplines that are easier for many people to accomplish and that can be equally effective. We call these time-out and isolation.

Scruff-Shake. When you catch the puppy in the act, like when you catch him jumping up on the table, take hold of his scruff under his ear and give a brief but brisk shake. If the puppy is small and has little loose skin under his ear (on the side of his neck), grasp his collar with your thumb and finger and give a quick shake. If the scruff-shake has been quick enough, your puppy should indicate, by ear position or by some degree of submission, that he understands that you don't like him jumping on the table (or chewing the lamp cord, etc.). But if he's merrily bouncing around with not a care in the world, you will know that the element of surprise and quickness wasn't there. If you find that this isn't a good discipline for you, don't use it. Others might be more suitable.

Put-Down. The put-down is a canine-type discipline for independent or dominant puppies, or for older puppies. It is definitely *not* for sensitive pups. It should be used only for serious problems. Perhaps a puppy has growled and shown his teeth. Again, the element of surprise and swiftness must be there. "No growling!" Reach for the puppy's collar, and push him immediately over on his side. Lean over him. You'll be down on your knees, but he will be in a forced submissive position, and you will be in a dominant position. In your deep, firm voice, tell him that growling is absolutely forbidden. Don't keep holding him down. Release him. If he's having a tantrum, keep him down until he settles, then let him up.

If the pup is misbehaving badly enough to need a scruff-shaking or a put-down, the discipline should not be followed immediately by praise. For example, when you catch him in the act of chewing a pillow, or when he growls at you, the discipline must be given quickly, and the pup must be ignored for several minutes with no petting or praise. After this period of time, you can speak to him quietly but with a firm voice. Whatever you do, don't apologize.

If you find that you are using either the scruff-shake or the put-down frequently, like several times a week, you must evaluate your relationship with your pup. Is he getting enough exercise? Are you spending enough time with him on a one-to-one basis? If you are using the canine-type disciplines often, then they are ineffective and shouldn't be used at all. Don't hesitate to call your breeder or another experienced person for advice.

Other canine disciplines might be more effective for you. These are a natural follow-through from the antisocial behavior that the pup might have experienced in the litter. When a puppy is playing too roughly with his teeth, the puppy that is being chewed on gives a screech and moves away. He won't play anymore. We can imitate this behavior.

Isolation. Isolation is effective because it's an immediate reaction the instant the pup misbehaves. A pup is a very social creature, and you are its adult pack member. If you totally withdraw all attention, he's going to be a very unhappy pup. So — when he's very mouthy and grabs at you when you pet him — say "off" or "no bite," and *immediately* turn your back to him. Fold your arms tightly, and even close your eyes. *Do not talk.* If he starts to jump on you or if he starts to bark, totally ignore him. Walk away and leave the room if necessary. The pup should feel totally isolated from you. After about a minute, unfreeze and say "hi" to your puppy. Tell him that he's a good puppy at that moment, and that you hope that he will continue to be good. Pat him again, and if his mouth starts chewing on you, repeat the isolation. And, of course, repeat the resultant quiet praise. It may take several repetitions in succession, but he should soon get the message.

Time-Out. The other method is called time-out. When your pup is doing something that you don't like — such as grabbing and chewing your pant leg — leave the room for a minute or two, or pick up the pup and take him to a time-out room (such as a bathroom or the kitchen). In a minute or two, let him back in, telling him what a good puppy he is. For extra-lively pups, divert their attention from the previous activity with a toy when they come back in. When you use time-out, don't just go off and leave him there, because then it won't be a learning situation for the pup. Bring the pup back in, and repeat the time-out if necessary.

Squirt Bottles. Many owners have success using squirt bottles for discipline. It interrupts the pup in the midst of barking or jumping up or grabbing at hands, and at the same time, the pup hears the "Quiet!", or "No Bark!", or "Off" command, followed by praise when he is no longer doing that behavior. Water bottles work well for a few times, but then puppies tend to treat the water squirt as a game. A most effective spray is a mild vinegar solution (one part vinegar to six parts water). Vinegar seems to be universally distasteful and therefore a successful inhibitor of certain behaviors for puppies from about four months old on through adulthood.

The Sit Command. This command is an important part of the disciplinary process. You have given your "No!" command to stop the behavior, followed immediately with "Sit!" to get the pup to respond to you. This is effective because you have not only stopped the bad behavior, you have also given the pup an alternative behavior for which he can then be praised. Obviously, the pup needs to know the sit command well enough to be able to respond to it under varying circumstances.

Evaluating the Different Disciplines

Domesticating a puppy involves continual interaction between two individual living beings — the puppy and the owner. We must acknowledge the fact that problems can be principally with the owners as much as with the puppy. In analyzing the effect of your teaching methods with your puppy, ask yourself: Is this particular method effective? If not, is *any* method working? If not, then what is wrong?

At this point, take an objective look at your personality and at your pup's personality. Is your pup growing up differently than you had anticipated? Do you sometimes think that you're a mismatch? Puppies go through many phases before they mature. Often, if you patiently keep on doing what you're doing, the pup will grow out of that particularly difficult stage of behavior. Encourage and praise the behaviors that make you happy. Distract or discourage the behaviors that you don't like. This is the way in which you can mold your pup's personality.

When you are evaluating, you must also be aware that there may be an underlying physical or functional abnormality causing the pup's difficult or seemingly intractable behavior. Have your pup checked out by a veterinarian before you proceed.

Puppies Will Be Puppies

There's the possibility that the new owner will exaggerate the degree of the behavior problem of a puppy. Especially with a first puppy, the owner may not realize that some digging, some chewing, some barking, and some jumping up are natural. This is why we keep stressing that it's up to the owner to teach the puppy what to do and what not to do. Puppies are canids, and there are certain behaviors that are simply not wrong from the puppy's point of view. So don't get angry at the pup just because you decide that he should act more like a person than a dog. Simply get busy and show him what you want him to do and what you don't want him to do.

Molding your pup's behavior isn't done in a day or two. It takes weeks of praising good behavior and discouraging bad behavior. It's a style of living, a daily program. Repeating your lesson in as many new places as you can will help you and your puppy learn to live together. Lessons learned at home will need to be repeated elsewhere so that the puppy learns what behavior you want and not just that the rules apply in your own house.

Accept your puppy as he is, not as you think he should be. If your pup is shy, it won't help for you to get stern and impatient. Accept the shyness and do what needs to be done. This also applies to the independent puppy and the assertive puppy. Over a period of weeks, you'll find that confidence and communication between the two of you are increasing and that your pup's general behavior is changing to fit your desires.

CHAPTER 8

DEVELOPMENT FROM THREE TO SIX MONTHS

This is an age to enjoy — but watch out! Your puppy is NOT too good to be true.

The rapid changes noticeable in the puppy's behavior during the first three months have leveled off. The central nervous system is now well-developed. By three months of age, the pup's problem-solving ability is functioning well, but his immaturity gets in the way. In other words, he has a short attention span and is too rambunctious to settle down and learn complicated behavior. However, he's certainly ready to learn simple commands (as discussed in Chapter 6).

This a delightful age and passes much too quickly. By the end of this period, the large-breed pups have grown to approximately two-thirds of their mature size, and small breeds may be close to their final height. After six months of age, the puppy will become much more independent, will reach sexual maturity, and will be very responsive to physiological stimuli. However, the age from three to six months is still one of puppy charm and innocence. The pup and people are adjusting to each other, and the pup is learning what the pack rules are. He's readily able to cope with life by now, he's a willing worker, and he is happy to try whatever you ask (at least most of the time).

Taking the pup to different places continues to be important at this age. The pup's environmental awareness is at a peak now. He's ready for anything. Exposure to a variety of places will continue to be a factor in building self-confidence in the puppy and will help him take stressful events in the future in his stride.

The second set of teeth begins to appear during this period, which can cause chewing and biting problems. The puppy needs some items of his own for chewing.

Dominance and Submission

By four months of age, the pup is beginning to show signs of dominance and submissiveness toward other dogs. Previously, we noted that a young puppy shouldn't be left with irritable older dogs because the puppy wouldn't recognize the dominance signs of the older dog and wouldn't respond with a sign of submission. As a consequence, the pup might get bitten. However, around four months of age, this changes, and the pup becomes aware that dominance is displayed by direct eye contact, by a tail held straight up and tightly moving, by a growl and showing of the front teeth, and by the dominant dog's putting his head over the shoulder area of the other dog.

The submissive signs that the pup will display toward a dominant dog are a flattening of the ears, tucking the tail between the legs, and cowering, if not rolling over on the side or back. Usually, a puppy is submissive to an older dog, although in some instances a very assertive puppy will soon realize that he can be dominant to an especially submissive adult. With young dogs close in age, some pups will be dominant over others, and generally a dominant-

Young dogs display dominance by leaning over the other dog. Note erect ears and high tail.

Total submissiveness can be demonstrated to either another dog or a person. Note tucked tail and averted gaze.

submissive relationship is established very quickly. With some pups, it's a change-about situation as they take turns at dominance and submission.

Avoidance Period

Around four months of age, the pup will go through an avoidance period similar to the fear period experienced at eight weeks. The puppy becomes very hesitant about doing anything new and different and becomes quite suspicious of anything new that is brought into his home environment or of any new place that he might be visiting.

If your pup has a quiet personality, he may not respond as happily during training sessions, or he may seem hesitant and a little fearful if you take him to a new place. If this is the case, ease off the training routine. Make it fun; just enjoy being with your pup.

On the other hand, if you have a very independent or assertive pup, this age may find him in a relatively receptive frame of mind. His being a little apprehensive of new things in his life will tend to make him look to you for support. While he's paying attention to you, get busy and teach him something.

Teething

In many breeds, there can be retention of puppy teeth during the period that permanent teeth are erupting. This can have a long-lasting effect in that the pathway that the permanent teeth will take if the puppy teeth are retained will be abnormal and may lead to permanent problems with the way in which the teeth close together. Another problem associated with retention of puppy teeth is damage to the surrounding gum, which may progress to chronic oral disease in adult life. Bearing in mind that the pup between four and five months is extra-sensitive, you should pay careful attention to the possibility of teething problems. If you have any doubts that teething is not going well, consult your veterinarian immediately.

The Pack Leader Concept

In the three- to six-month age period, the most important help that you can give your puppy is to let him know that you're the pack leader. This way, there will be no doubt in his mind. The loyalty shown by the dog to his master and family is a manifestation of pack behavior. You and your family are the pack to which your dog belongs, and the house and yard are his den and territory.

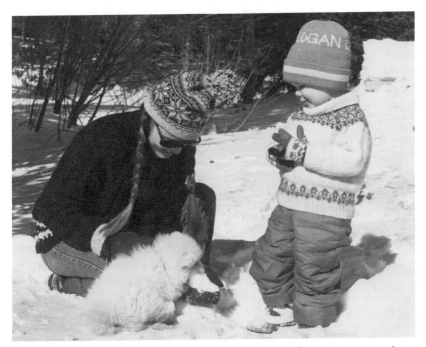

Becoming the pack leader begins as you expose the puppy to various activities and environments. *Photo by Kent Dannon.*

The dog is not a democratic animal. If you allow your pup an equal say in his activities, he will interpret that as an offer of pack leadership. He will begin to guide your activities to coincide with his benefits. He'll determine such things as where he wants to sleep, how often he wants to be let in and out of the house, and how much attention he gets. A dog with a more aggressive personality may even go to the extent of not letting you touch his food pan and of growling or snapping if you try to make him do something that he doesn't want to do.

An extremely important and necessary factor in raising a puppy is to establish yourself as the pack leader. This involves a conscious effort on your part. It's very easy to let these three months slide by and to think that *your* puppy doesn't need training because he's such a good dog. But in a few months, you'll regret that decision. The sweet puppy that never needed puppy training because he never did anything wrong begins to exercise his mature personality. He's not mean, but suddenly he's a lively handful that isn't paying any attention to you because the pattern of communication wasn't established as a puppy. This applies to the toy breeds as well as to the large breeds. Three to six months is a good age to reinforce your image as pack leader, because the pup still likes to be close to you, it's easy to get his attention, and he's easy to discipline.

The Pack Leader

Anyone who has been involved in maintaining a group of dogs together in a common environment will know that they establish a hierarchy or social order that has a pack leader. Because your dog is a dog, he is very aware of social order and will find his position sooner or later. In the family situation, many people automatically assume that they are the pack leader on the rather uncertain premise of human supremacy over animals. But are you *really* the pack leader, and does your dog know it? Many dog behavior problems can occur if you're not the pack leader.

Dogs can experience emotional reactions. They experience frustration when they don't know who is in control of their territory and when they don't know which of their actions are acceptable and which are not. Depending on the dog's personality, this uncertainty might manifest itself in the dog's taking over as pack leader to the point of growling and snapping or of urinating and defecating in the house (after he has been well house-trained). Frustration may also appear as destructive behavior, such as ripping furniture, excessive digging in the yard, or incessant barking.

We feel that it is vitally important for people to understand the pack-leader concept. Establishing the rules of the game can be done easily during puppyhood. It results in a dog that fits into the life-style of your home. If minor behavioral problems subsequently arise, they are relatively easy to deal with if you and the dog have developed a mutual respect.

The role of leader is abdicated by many people because they see it as the lion-tamer-with-a-whip concept, or as a dictator complex with no pleasant communication allowed. This is not the case at all. In a good dog-person relationship (with you as the pack leader), mutual respect is absolutely necessary. The person must respect the dog and must understand the physical and social needs unique to being a canid. On the other hand, the dog must respect you, and he will if he is treated with consistency and if he knows the rules that you have established are for the mutual benefit of man and dog. Dogs need guidelines and need to know the limits.

How Do You Become the Pack Leader?

It isn't a short-term battle of wills in which you are the victor and the puppy is vanquished. It is built on daily routine. Being the pack leader doesn't mean that you must be big and aggressive. A small woman can be the pack leader. It's an attitude — an air of authority. It's the basis for the mutual respect that is so important for building a bridge of communication between the two of you.

Many pack-leader activities are a part of the puppy training routine (which is discussed in detail in Chapter 11). "Sit" is the most important command that your pup can learn because it is so easy to use as a reminder that you're in charge of things. Tell the pup to "sit" before you feed him, before you play with him, and

Walking with a pup helps to put you in the place of pack leader. Periodically stop and call him to you.

before you let him go outside. This shows the pup that he must respond to you before he indulges in pleasure for himself and keeps him from becoming a spoiled brat.

As you're teaching him the sit, praise him with a pat on the chest, which is in itself a means of impressing your leadership position on the puppy. Leaning over is canine language for dominance. (In fact, if you have an especially sensitive or shy puppy, you may want to avoid leaning over the pup because it may intimidate him.)

Another good pack-leader exercise involves combining the come with taking the pup on a walk without a leash. For this, you should take the puppy to an area that's uncrowded, preferably with no people at all. Most three-month-old pups won't want to get too far away from you, which is another reason why this is a good age. Go for a walk together, and when the pup gets about twenty-five feet away, get his attention by calling his name and clapping your hands. When he looks at you, kneel down and call him to you. Give him lots of praise when he gets to you and continue your walk, repeating this another three or four times. If you have an independent puppy that ignores you, try running away from him. Many pups can't resist that and will follow. If you have a *very* independent puppy, begin calling him when he's just ten feet away and give him a very small piece of cheese or some other good treat as soon as he gets to you. This exercise reminds the puppy that you're always there and that you're the leader who must be reported to every so often.

You'll be accepted as pack leader by your dog when you're consistent and fair in your demands. For example, if you let the pup jump up on you one day and then the next day you kick or slap him for doing the same thing, the pup will be confused and will wonder when he can do something and when not.

The aspiring pack leader doesn't permit the puppy to growl or snap at him. A severe scruff-shaking is necessary when this happens, followed by no attention from you for ten to fifteen minutes. A growl or a snap is not unusual behavior for many pups. It's a natural way for them to show irritation. Usually one or two corrections are all that's necessary to eliminate that behavior. However, if the pup is not corrected, you're asking for big trouble later.

Give some thought as to what stimulus provoked the growl or the snap. If the pup has been treated unnecessarily roughly, it's up to you to change the situation.

How Does a Dog Become the Pack Leader?

Very easily. He's either ignored most of the time or overindulged and smothered with attention. He isn't trained. He isn't taught the difference between good and bad and so he establishes his own criteria with himself as the center of attention. As a result, he may become not very pleasant for you or your friends and neighbors to live with. It's supposed to be the other way around — the dog is living in *your* world. Someone has to call the shots and both you and your dog will be happier if it's you.

Conclusion

Guide the puppy to behave the way you want him to from the time you bring him home. Be patient. Behavior development takes time. If you're relaxed and don't turn every act of your puppy into a major battle, you'll find that having a puppy in the house is one of the most delightful experiences you've ever had and that having a mature dog in the house that respects you is deeply rewarding.

Photo by Joyce Woolley.

CHAPTER 9

THE IMPORTANCE
OF PERSONALITY

*"Accept your puppy as he is, then mold
the kind of dog you want."*

Sometimes it's very difficult to see your pup as he really is, rather than as you want him to be. Exuberant, forceful people cannot really believe that their pup might be a little short of confidence and need morale-boosting. Quiet people have difficulty believing that their pup is leader-oriented and must have a firm hand and firm voice. Surely, this assertive little puppy will become sweet and gentle any day now — wishing will make it so. The fact is, you must accept the pup the way he is and then proceed to mold the kind of adult dog you want.

Individual Characteristics

The pup's individual genetic qualities determine factors such as the degree of shyness or aggressiveness and other traits such as curiosity and excitability. These traits are found in all breeds, purebred and mongrel alike, and are components in a dog's personality. What is the basic temperament of your puppy? Is he dependent, independent, leader-oriented, aggressive, eager to please, shy, or too easily excited? As the pack leader, you will continue to develop a communication with your pup by training him. This needs to be done according to the pup's personality, however, or the training can do more harm than good at this age.

The Dependent Puppy

This pup is usually found in the toy breeds. He looks to his owner for approval for all of his actions and tends to be emotional. This pup wants constantly to stay very close to his owner and does a minimum of investigating. It's very easy to get in the habit of carrying this puppy, an activity that should be limited because it will exaggerate the dog's dependency to the extent of making him overly nervous. Gentleness is needed in living with this pup. Keep showing the pup what you expect him to do, and he'll soon respond. Don't treat this pup like a baby. That will make him an emotional cripple. Just because he's small and acts very dependent upon you doesn't mean that he can't learn good puppy behavior.

The Independent Puppy

A little independence is a good thing. There is nothing wrong with having a puppy that thinks for himself at times, but some pups are more inclined this way than others. The sign of a very independent puppy is to not be able to get his attention to come to you when you are only six feet away calling him. This pup will ignore your voice and your hand clapping and will sniff along, going his own merry way. If this pup isn't given puppy training, he will be difficult to train as an adult because his desire to please will by then be focused mostly on himself. This pup takes patience and firmness but generally is easy to train because the dog is calm and not emotional.

Use a cord to keep the independent puppy under control during the training sessions so that he can never not come when called.

If it's possible, keep the pup in a dog crate or in a room or yard area by himself for at least thirty minutes before the training session. This will help to encourage his attention to you. If at first he seems more interested in everything else than in you, be patient and show him firmly what you want him to do. Reward him with a pat on the chest or with your voice, saying, "Good dog," or both. You may want to use tidbits to get his attention. The trick is to keep his attention zeroed in on you. Keep sessions short and be aware that it might take many of them before your pup responds like you want him to.

The Eager-to-Please Puppy

This pup will respond to your voice very quickly and will eagerly come running to you when you call him (from close distances, of course). It will seem as though he learns very quickly because he wants to do what you show him to do. He's so responsive to you that it's easy to mistake this and think that he already knows how to sit or come or stay. However, this pup needs much repetition and will take almost as long to actually learn something as the more independent puppy. This is probably the easiest type to work with. Training sessions can be for longer periods without stressing the puppy. But to begin with, no pup should have more than five minutes at a time. These pups are filled with charm and will train you readily to their desires, so watch for this.

The Shy Puppy

This pup has some distinctive behavioral patterns. He may crouch and freeze when you approach him. He may be overly sensitive. He may cringe and stay away if you raise your voice even a little. He may be very fearful in a new place, even though there are no noises or other frightening things. He may not want to approach another person even though the person is quiet and nonfrightening. Some pups will roll on their sides or urinate when you show them attention. This is also an indication of excessive submission.

Guide the puppy gently but firmly to do what you want him to do, then follow a couple of minutes of working with a short play period. Improvement will be slow, but it will come. The pup may not want to participate in learning any of the commands such as sit or come or stay, but keep repeating the learning sessions with lots of patience.

You must be the pack leader for this puppy also. If you're not, the pup will take over the job. He can see that he has you trained to let him act the way he wants. For example, if you feel sorry for this pup when he starts to act shy and frightened and you begin to pet him, you are rewarding his behavior and encouraging him to act that way in the future. Instead, when he begins to act shy,

A pup showing signs of submissiveness.

speak to him in a pleasant, firm voice, but don't pet him until his behavior is more what you want it to be, even if for only a split second. It is especially important to make the training sessions fun. Keep his mind on you and off himself.

This pup was born with a short supply of confidence, and he will need a lot of patience from you. His behavior will gradually improve as your pup gets confidence in himself and in you.

The Dominant Puppy That Competes for Pack Leadership

The dominant-aggressive pup is a very active one and demands a lot of attention. He's little and cute, and it's very easy to give him all of the attention that he wants. He becomes spoiled because of the overindulgence. Then the aggressive tendency shows up as he grows older and you don't want to cater to him anymore. He will let you know that he's unhappy with you.

The competitive puppy might snap at you if you reach down to move his feed pan while he's eating, or he may snap at you during leash training if he decides that he doesn't want to stay at your side. In other words, the pup will try to do things his way, and if you permit this, you are setting yourself up for serious, difficult behavior as he gets older. Aggressive actions in the puppy cannot be permitted. We can't stress strongly enough the importance of not allowing the aggressive puppy to become the dominant member of the relationship.

When the pup snaps at you, it will be a shock and a surprise, but don't retreat, because this is what he wants. This rewards his snapping and encourages him to do it again. Use a severe scruff-shake or be prepared with a squirt bottle of vinegar water. When this type of puppy needs to be disciplined, he shouldn't be slapped or beaten, because he might take it as a challenge and fight back.

Puppy training is essential for the leader-oriented pup. It teaches him that he receives a reward for obeying, for submitting to your commands. Teach the pup the sit command and use it constantly. This keeps reminding the pup that you're the boss.

The Extremely Excitable Puppy

All puppies can become excited easily, but some won't calm down. Some you can hardly touch because they are constantly wiggling. Such a pup will really try your patience. He's difficult

The curious puppy is always busy. *Photo by Kent Dannon.*

to work with because you can't get his attention for more than a few seconds. You may need to start with sessions that are less than a minute long. They can gradually become longer as the pup learns to pay attention. Try not to add to his excitement by any quick motions on your part. Stay calm with as little body movement as possible. Keep repeating the training routine. Don't pet him or tell him that he's a good dog until you've finished the training session. Sometimes it helps if the pup is allowed to run off some of his energy in a supervised enclosure before the training lesson begins. Then put the leash on and tell him that school is in session.

If over a period of time you've tried the puppy training routine every day and you see no improvement, there may be a physiological reason for the pup's behavior. In a few cases, some pups are so excitable that you can't hold their attention long enough to even begin training. These are signs of overexcitability, in which case you should get the help of a veterinarian. Certain dogs have a problem similar to hyperactive children and respond to similar treatment. If you think that this might be the case, discuss it with your veterinarian.

The Trainer's Personality

Your personality is also a factor in puppy training. If you are very shy — or quite assertive — this may indeed affect your pup's reactions to you. Be aware of how you are coming across to your pup. If necessary, moderate your approach. Usually, though, a pup will adjust to your individual personality and will want to do things your way as long as you're consistent and he knows what you want him to do. Within the bounds of respecting your pup and not abusing him, your method of dog training should be what seems natural to you. It's up to you to decide if you're being too tough on your pup or too lenient. Be honest with yourself. Open your eyes. Your pup is continually telling you how things really are and what kind of training he needs from you. Puppy training is a one-on-one proposition. Trust your instincts. Listen to your pup; read his body language. He can tell you a lot more than your neighbor can.

As different as breed and genetic characteristics might be in a population of puppies, almost any one of them, if given adequate socialization, can learn to respond to humans in a very satisfactory way.

Photo by Richard Piliero.

CHAPTER 10

BEHAVIORAL PROBLEMS

Don't let your pup learn bad habits! That's the cardinal
rule of the right start.

You have probably noticed that your pup has behavioral problems in which he specializes. Some puppies seem to have a prefer-
ence in where they want to channel their mischief. In this chapter,
we will talk about ideas for dealing with specific puppy behaviors
that you want to stop. You can and should expect your pup to
learn good behavior!

Most behavioral problems are caused by boredom and isolation.
This is why we say that it is essential to spend time every day with
your pup and have him with you in the house or in the yard while
you're home. When you're not home, the pup should not be loose

111

in the house but should be either in a crate, in a small puppy-proof room, or in an outdoor pen.

Prevention of Behavioral Problems

A few problem behaviors don't become noticeable until the pup reaches adolescence. By that time, it's more difficult to deal with the problem than it would have been to prevent it earlier. When problem behaviors do appear in earlier puppyhood, start dealing with them right away. Don't put them off and hope that they will go away, because in all probability, they will just get worse. Fortunately, strategies for prevention of problems involve very little time and are easily incorporated into activity time that you would already be spending with your pup.

Guarding the Food Dish

All family members should work on the food-dish exercise at one time or another. This exercise not only prevents your pup from becoming protective of his food, it also accustoms him to having hands come close to his face. This is important if there are children in the family.

There are three things that you can do while your puppy is eating. Begin by putting tidbits into his dish, one at a time, until he's accustomed to your hand reaching out toward his dish. The treat should be something special, such as raw hamburger or pieces of hot dog. You want him to associate a hand in his food dish with something very pleasant. After he has become very comfortable with your hand in his dish, touch his pan, moving it out of position. Finally, pick up his dish and set it back down. If your pup is starting to guard his toys, offer a tidbit while you take his bone or toy from him. This conditions him to accepting your hand. If he growls at any time use a vigorous scruff-shake or vinegar squirt bottle, and give a "No!"

Jumping Out of Reach

It's very natural for a puppy to scoot out of reach when you bend over to take him by the collar. Use a yummy tidbit for this also. Whenever you call your puppy to you, give him a treat with

Reach out and scratch your pup under the ears at every opportunity. This is especially important for both the timid and the dominant puppy because it removes their sense of being threatened when a hand comes towards them.

one hand while the other hand touches his collar. In this way, he'll be comfortable with your hand reaching for his collar. Be sure that your pup comes all the way to you before he receives his treat — don't reach out to him.

Separation Distress

Conditioning your pup to being left home alone can prevent serious problems. If not attended to, separation distress can develop into separation anxiety, which is often expressed by frantic barking and destructiveness. In extreme cases, this can involve furniture or even walls and doors. Conditioning your pup to being left home alone can avoid these problems as your pup grows older. We periodically meet with dog owners who have this problem. It could have been avoided by dealing with this distress when the pup was young, which is the easy time to work with it. Otherwise, by the time a dog reaches adolescence, it is a serious problem indeed.

If your puppy has had constant attention since he first arrived at your home, and then you suddenly leave him home alone, he can experience a state of isolation that results in fear and panic. Therefore, you need to help your pup learn to be comfortable by himself. Teaching the pup that it's okay to be alone should be done while *you're* at home, too. If the pup is to be left in a small room or the backyard while you're gone, put him there occasionally while you're at home working around the house.

Begin with short separation periods of five minutes. If he's barking when you're ready to return to him, try to wait until he has stopped (at least long enough to take a breath), then open the door. Gradually increase the length of time before you return.

The manner in which you leave the house and later return to your puppy is also a factor in how he perceives your absence. If you're emotional and feel guilty about leaving him, he'll sense this and will become nervous and upset. Practice your arrivals and departures at the same time you're conditioning him to your absence. When you leave him, don't be emotional — no petting or special fun games. Such handling followed immediately by separation can result in more intense separation distress. Keep your departure low-key. You can speak to your pup and tell him that you're leaving, then leave. Use the same phrase every time you leave; for example, "Be a good dog; I'll be back." When you arrive home, greet your pup warmly but briefly and go about your business. Later, when you have time, you can have a play period, take a walk, or whatever.

If your absences are occasional and are for no more than a few hours at a time, the pup's crate is ideal and should not result in distress because that's his den and he is accustomed to it. But all puppies should be taught that they can stay home alone for longer periods of time. Try to have a larger safe area for your puppy if you'll be gone longer than a few hours. Make sure that there's a place where he can eliminate and a shelter place in case of bad weather if he's outdoors.

Digging

There's no magic answer here. It's not your puppy's fault that you have a perfectly landscaped backyard. Sniffing and digging in the dirt are naturally doggy things to do, especially for puppy dogs.

If you can't be out with the pup all the time to distract him when he begins digging, fix a fenced area where he is free to dig all he desires. When you see him digging in another part of the lawn, take him to his own area. Some pups will learn to like digging in their own place, especially if there's a hole already started or the ground is soft. Most puppies outgrow digging, but some mature dogs will periodically dig all their lives. The earth is cool, and the burying of bones is a strong impulse with them. Boredom is another continuing cause of digging.

Specific Behavioral Problems

Chewing

Puppies chew for three reasons: they are bored and want something to do, they have too much energy from not enough exercise, and/or they are teething and have sore gums. You will need to teach your puppy that chewing on his toys is the only chewing allowed. This is the process that we call molding your pup's behavior and is discussed in the previous chapter. For many puppies, this keeps problem chewing to a minimum; however, there's always an item or two around the house that they can't resist, and there is also that percentage of pups that are exceptionally mouthy.

For problem chewers, a bad taste often inhibits the chewing desire. Try Bitter Apple™, available in pet-supply stores, or try very hot Chinese or Mexican pepper sauce. Listerine© and its aroma can be a repellant to pups. Test the furniture or other pieces with a small amount to be certain that no discoloration occurs. Puppies are very sensitive to a distasteful substance and should quickly associate that with the item on which it has been applied. Keep applying the substance until the puppy is no longer testing the area to see if the taste has changed. Be consistent!

Puppies are at their worst between four to six months of age, during the teething process, but the problem can continue periodically for several more months. Some pups find relief with chewing an ice cube or a frozen rawhide chip. To avoid serious chewing damage, never give your pup the run of the house. He should either be with you so that you can monitor his chewing, or he should be confined. Tether the pup to you with a leash or other cord. Then he can be with you when you're too busy to keep track of him all the time. Too many valuables have been ruined because the pup's owner wanted to be "nice."

Barking

Now is the time to develop a pattern of control for barking. This is probably one of the most frustrating problems facing a dog owner. It can create enemies of neighbors and can result in warnings and fines from dog-control agencies — and justifiably so. Any dog that won't stop barking for long periods of time is causing much distress for numerous innocent people and is contributing to anti-dog sentiment. The responsible dog owner begins avoiding this problem by training his puppy to the quiet command.

Barking is a natural canine activity. There's no reason to expect a dog never to bark, but you *can* expect him to learn to stop barking. The shake can is a good way to accomplish this. When the pup has barked a few times, give the quiet command, *then* shake the can until the barking stops. The noise should startle the puppy into silence, at which point you immediately praise him! The pup will likely begin barking again, and you will repeat the procedure as many times as necessary until the pup doesn't return to barking. Always give the command first, then the distraction. *Always* praise the pup as soon as he stops barking.

You also might want to attract him away from where he is barking so that you can achieve success with the quiet command. This is an ongoing process. Some pups learn the quiet command quickly, while others have regular relapses. As with many other aspects of puppy behavior, you automatically work on the problem every time it occurs until you reach a point where you say, "Wow, he's learning that command really well!"

The puppy that is barking outside at night shouldn't be outside all night. He should be in the house, in a crate or in a secure area.

The cause of some barking problems is similar to the cause of some excessive chewing and digging problems — not enough time spent with the puppy, and not enough exercise for the puppy.

Jumping Up

One serious behavioral problem is when the pup — or the dog — jumps on or chases children. Young children have an erratic gait, which can trigger an automatic chase response in the dog's brain. Therefore, he must be taught that this is forbidden. The off command (which means to keep all feet off of humans) can be used for this. Use it consistently whenever the pup tries to jump on anybody. Eventually, the off command, when used at an appropriate time, will stop the pup before he jumps.

You will need to help your pup understand what this command means. When the pup jumps on you, give a quick shake with his collar as you say "Off!" As soon as he's on the floor, tell him that he's a good puppy. Be ready to repeat this several times in a row if necessary. For the larger or older pup, catch the front feet as he jumps, give an off command, then hold him up on his hind feet a few seconds. Praise him after he's back on the floor.

The ideal method, once your puppy knows the sit command, is to tell him to sit, then give him a treat or a pat as soon as his bottom touches down. Isolation often works well with this, too. When he jumps, say "Off!" then turn away and fold your arms across your chest, totally ignoring the puppy. Praise and pet him when he's down on the floor. Don't wait until your pup has jumped on you, then gotten down, to praise good behavior. Give him pats and praise when he's with you and is *not* jumping.

To teach the pup about jumping on children, have the pup on his leash, or make a long line out of clothes line or other cord. Tie the leash around your waist or through your belt. This ensures that you will have instant control for correcting your pup's behavior. Set aside a time for this activity during a play period. When your child comes close and the pup starts to run and jump, give the off command, followed by a quick tug on the leash. Then take hold of the collar and give a brisk shake. Praise him as soon as he's on the ground and being good. If he immediately jumps up, repeat the correction and then the praise.

After your pup begins to understand and is seldom jumping up as long as he's tied to you, continue the training by letting the leash drag on the ground. You will be staying close. As soon as he behaves, praise him with "you're a good dog," and walk near the child again. You may need three or four corrections in succession before the pup settles down. You will also need to repeat this setup for several days in succession and again in about a week.

The child must also be taught how to behave — no screaming or shouting or waving the arms around.

Mouthiness and Biting

A dog feels the world through his mouth. The mouth — the teeth, the cheeks, and the tongue — is a tactile area. If you watch a mature dog, you might see him mouth an item to identify it or understand it. With your puppy, this natural tendency can sometimes get out of hand. If the pup were still in the litter or playing with other dogs, he would be told when he was biting or mouthing too hard. Now that the pup is living in your pack, you will replace the interaction that the pup would have with the other pups and dogs. You must step in and continue with bite-inhibition training in a manner that is perceived as normal by your puppy.

Teach your pup the stop-it or no-bite command. When he nips at you, take him by the collar and look him in the eye for several seconds while you repeat the command. Release him and in a few seconds tell him quietly that he's a good puppy. Reach out to touch him, and if he starts playing with his mouth again, repeat the correction.

Another effective correction is to isolate the pup — totally ignore him as soon as you say "No bite!" Fold your arms, and don't even look at him. After a couple of minutes, give your pup another chance to play with you. Repeat the isolation routine as often as necessary until he moderates his mouthiness.

Occasionally, a puppy owner needs to wear a glove to help teach the pup about biting. With a glove, you can keep your hand movements slow and calm. Often it is the jerky hand movements (because of the sharp teeth) that excite the puppy and keep him grabbing the hand in play.

The glove can also be used to teach your pup the easy or the gentle command so that you can put your hand in the pup's mouth and he won't bite down. *All puppies must learn this command, whatever their breed.*

The Aggressive Puppy

Occasionally, there is a pup that bites not in play but out of fear or dominance aggression. This demands a big "NO" with

All pups should learn
the "gentle" or
"easy" command.
Photo by Jane Exon.

your voice. The swiftness of the correction is imperative. Do not talk to the pup after this correction for several minutes.

In the adult dog, aggression is the single most serious behavioral problem with veterinarians and trainers. It's normal for a pup to have an aggressive reaction to some action that he perceives as threatening to him.

However, we emphasized previously that early socialization is very important in familiarizing your puppy with the variety of circumstances that he will encounter in life. If your puppy has had a well-balanced relationship with his littermates until weaning, this bodes well for his ability to interact with dogs in the future. If your puppy has been handled kindly by yourself and by other members of the family — young and old, male and female — this bodes well for future transactions with people. Subsequently, as the puppy passes through the period of environmental awareness (nine to twelve weeks), his understanding of dominance and submission is enhanced. He becomes increasingly aware of his environment and really begins to appreciate what a neat person you are. Finding and establishing the right balance of dominant and submissive behavior throughout these stages will result in a more confident and socially well-adjusted puppy. These are the puppies that will be less likely to give you problems with aggressive behavior. In fact, many of the early problems with fear and dominance-cued aggression will be reduced or prevented by your diligently following the full socialization program.

The pup must learn that any aggressive act will be totally inhibited. Certain cues, such as rapid movement of hands toward the pup, can elicit an aggressive response. These pups must be conditioned to hand movement immediately. With a tidbit in one hand, let the pup nibble and lick while the other hand moves toward the pup's ear. If the pup stops nibbling and eyes the hand, move the hand back. Keep moving forward with one hand (the other is holding the tidbit in front of the pup's mouth) until you can scratch behind the ear and pet the pup. Then reverse hands and repeat the same procedure. At this point, it is essential to teach the gentle, or easy, command, beginning with the gloved hand and progressing to putting your bare hand in the mouth. If this isn't done during the puppy months, very serious problems lie ahead. In addition, puppy training is essential for this pup. This builds self-confidence in the fearful pup and develops an appropriate relationship with the dominant puppy.

Be Creative

No book can possibly cover all of the various and unique problems that puppies present. As you get to know your puppy, you will learn what types of disciplines are more effective, as well as what types of distractions work best. You can utilize this knowledge to determine your own ideas for behavioral problems. Adolescent puppies can certainly keep us on our toes when it comes to staying one jump ahead of their busy minds.

Perhaps your pup is jumping up and getting things off of the kitchen counter. You need to stop this behavior immediately. If you can catch him at it the first times he tries it, your chances of extinguishing the behavior are very good. Use your imagination and think of a setup that will startle him. For example, put some food on a piece of newspaper on the counter. Stack some empty cans around the back and sides of the food. When his paws get on the counter, the paper will move, which will send the cans tumbling. At the same time, you're going to appear from behind a door, saying, "No! Off!" After he's been impressed with the results of his behavior, you can tell him that you much prefer him to keep all of his feet on the floor, and that he's a good boy when he does that.

Teaching your pup the rules of the house is an ongoing, day-by-day process. The weeks of teaching good manners can be very rewarding as you watch the pup blossom with a sense of confidence. The weeks will also be filled with humor and good times, and the occasional times of total frustration will be kept to a minimum.

Here's a suggestion. When you do reach a point of frustration, give some thought to the various aspects of the pup's irritating behavior. Where do your actions fit in? Your pup is acting in accordance with his dog genes. It's your responsibility to understand this and to understand his need for consistency in your behavior. After all, you're the mature, reasoning individual in this growing relationship — aren't you?

Photo by Robert Spanner.

Photo by Paulette Braun.

CHAPTER 11

THE JOYS OF PUPPY TRAINING

The one most important factor in raising and training a puppy from three to six months of age is getting the puppy to pay attention to you.

Just as the mature canids show their pups how to pay attention and how to behave in the pack, so now the human must show the pup how to pay attention and behave as a new member of the human pack. This is puppy training — teaching a pup how to be a happy, cooperative member of his human pack.

You may think that this training isn't necessary for *your* pup. He's so attentive and does everything that you want him to do. Please, take it on faith that he needs to learn the basics of how to concentrate and how to do basic tasks on command while it's still easy for you both. When your pup is around six months of age and older, he'll want to do *what* he wants to do and *when* he wants to do it. If you have a communication system going by then, you'll be able to minimize some of the major frustrations, such as running through the house, jumping on people and furniture, tracking every interesting smell, and, most of all, ignoring you. Female pups are just as good at this as males.

Communicating with Your Puppy

The tasks that you teach in puppy training are the foundation for communication as your puppy ventures into adolescence. You want to bring out the best in your puppy. You want him to relate to you, to your family, to your veterinarian, and to your friends. The basis for a relationship between you and your puppy is built through the use of your hands, your eyes, your voice, and the leash.

Using Hands for Communication
The first contact with human hands is in the whelping box, where the pup is picked up and handled as part of the daily routine — with a certain amount of cuddling, too. These hands move with confidence, and the stroking gives the puppy a feeling of security.

After you take the pup to your home, your hands will calm the puppy, warm him, play with him, and let him know that he can have confidence in his new pack home. However, as the pack leader, you must take care that his attitude toward hands doesn't change. Hands sometimes come at the puppy too often and too abruptly (especially if there are children in the family), and the pup might growl or snap or shy away. To prevent this, you can teach your puppy that hands are okay, that even though the movement might be quick and startling, these are human hands and should be accepted as a fact of life. You are also responsible to see that the pup is never *abused* by hands.

The way in which you use your hands during the pup's socialization determines how that pup will react to your hands. He has to learn how to read your hand movements. To begin conditioning your pup to hand movements, use tiny tidbits. Have them in your

Continue to use voice and hand communication as your puppy grows. Keep the pup's attention on you. Use your voice. Pat your leg.

Get your pup's attention the moment he becomes distracted. *Photos by Joyce Woolley.*

pocket, and occasionally when your pup is close to you, offer a tidbit. While he is sniffing and taking it, reach out for his collar with your other hand, or touch his ear, or pat him on the head. As he gets accustomed to taking tidbits, move your hand more quickly. Each member of the family should do this individually.

When you begin teaching basic commands such as the sit, become very aware of where that hand is. Does it stay in the appropriate position, or does it wave about randomly as though the hand muscles are not under your control? Many of you will be surprised to find how erratic your hand movements are — over and around and anywhere but next to the pup's lips and nose — which is where your hand should be when you begin the teaching process. Any other movement can be distracting or confusing to the pup. The details of hand position and movement will be discussed in the instructions for teaching the various tasks.

Using Your Eyes for Communication

Eye contact in the wolf pack is one of the ways of keeping order. Only the alpha animals (male or female) use it, to remind the others of who's in charge and, in general, to maintain the status quo of the leader. To a certain extent, this is also the purpose for human-dog eye contact. When you initiate eye contact, you express your alpha position. The difference is that you don't expect your pup to turn away or avert his eyes. You will encourage your pup to maintain eye contact for several seconds, and you will make it a pleasant experience.

Use the term "watch me," or use his name to teach eye contact. You can make a noise to get his attention, wiggle your fingers up beside your eye, or move a tidbit from his nose to your eye until he understands what you want. Always praise him the instant you have eye contact — that is how he learns what you want. If you have trouble getting your pup to look at you, take his muzzle (or whole head) in your hands, and turn his head up toward you. Praise him the instant your eyes connect, then release him. A very submissive dog will have a hard time maintaining eye contact, so give him lots of encouragement. A dominant pup won't want to make eye contact on your terms, but keep working at it and praise him vigorously when he gives you even a momentary glance.

The "Watch Me" command focuses your pup's attention on you. *Photo by Jane Exon.*

Be calm and confident when you ask for eye contact. Smiling is okay. Stand up straight. You're asking for your pup's respect, so don't get down on his level for this. Read your puppy's eyes.

Continually use eye contact — in the house, on walks, whenever. The pup that grows up never having established a pattern of eye contact will become a dog that is not readily trainable, and he will have trouble learning good manners.

The watch me command teaches your pup that you want his attention — that you want him to check in with you. Therefore, it can be followed by a command such as "sit," or "this way," or it can be followed by a "good dog" and a pat on the head or shoulder. You've gotten your pup's attention — you're happy and he's happy. As you continue to get eye contact and to keep it for longer than a few seconds, you'll be delighted at your pup's expressions and at how beautiful his eyes are. That feeling seems to be mutual.

Using Your Voice for Communication

Throughout all the other aspects of puppy training, your voice is the one constant — the one prevailing influence on your puppy's basic attitude toward you. The tone of your voice can aid your puppy's blossoming sense of confidence or it can keep him watching you out of the corners of his eyes, wondering when harshness is going to strike again. The opposite of harshness is equally disturbing to a puppy but in a different way. A high-pitched baby-talk tone of voice can keep a puppy confused. He perceives that as an emotional tone, one similar to early tones of his littermates. We have seen puppy behavior settle down considerably when the owner slowed down the word flow and lowered her voice.

A growly voice when you're disciplining your pup, a happy voice when you're praising your pup, and a firm, calm voice when you're training your pup are all natural, and all make sense to your puppy. He learns to know which tone goes with which of his behaviors, and this knowledge greatly speeds the molding of his behavior. This, indeed, is puppy training.

Using the Leash for Communication

Most dog owners don't think of the leash as a means of communication. They see it as an item to prevent the pup from wandering off. But think about this. How much time will your dog, during his life, spend at the other end of the leash? Most of you probably live in communities that have a leash law. Therefore, unless you know of some open space where your dog can run loose (and we hope that you do), your dog will spend a great amount of time walking and running on a leash or on a long line (marvelous for giving the pup twenty to thirty feet of roaming and still keep him under control).

Your pup's perception of you is determined in part by the way in which he is treated on the leash. If you're rough and inconsistent with jerks and pulls, your pup will be confused. In contrast, if your pup drags you wherever he wishes, he perceives you as letting him do whatever he wants. Neither of these attitudes is a basis for good communication. Look upon your leash as a training tool. The details for doing this are described later in this chapter.

Teaching Your Puppy to Learn

Puppy training isn't obedience training. The object of puppy training is to help your pup learn how to perform certain tasks, such as sit, come, down, and walk on a leash. The tasks themselves have a purpose beyond the performance by the puppy. We use them to teach the pup *how* to learn. This means getting all of his neurons sparking in the right order so that, as he matures, he will be able to process the steps of learning and will have the commands (vocabulary) to use as building blocks in learning other activities.

What else do we mean when we say that we are teaching a puppy how to learn? We teach the pup to look at us, to listen to us, and to concentrate for a few seconds. This results in his doing the task and in his receiving praise. The watching, listening, and concentrating skills are the skills that your pup will use all of his life, and they soon will be of great value as the pup grows into adolescence and becomes more independent. If puppy kindergarten classes are available in your community, we highly recommend this experience for you and your pup.

How to Proceed

Tidbits. In the morning when you get up, put tidbits in your pocket. When you get home from work, put tidbits in your pocket. And, on days off, keep tidbits in your pocket, because you never know when you will be using one. The nice thing about puppy training is that it can be done anywhere at anytime.

Guiding your pup with tidbits to sit, to down, to come, and to walk beside you is the quickest and most stress-free way to teach your pup. The valuable part about this type of training is that it teaches your puppy to pay attention to you at the same time that it teaches him to concentrate and to focus his attention on an action. The more he does it, the more he gets praised and the more his confidence grows. A good habit is thus formed.

These tidbits should be something that your pup *really* likes, not pieces of his dog food. Oven-baked liver (baked at 350 degrees for an hour and left in the oven to dry) is always exciting to pups.

Be sure to cut the liver into very small pieces. Thinly sliced hot dogs really get a pup's attention, too. Cheese is also popular. Try popcorn with garlic powder sprinkled on it. Various commercial treats are also enticing. It's well worth the effort to find something that your pup thinks is very exciting. For the pup that isn't a chow hound, you may have to teach him to like a tidbit. At mealtime, before you show him his supper, get him excited about the tidbit that you're holding and see if he'll take it from your fingers. Toss a piece into his food bowl. All puppies can be convinced that a tidbit is a great thing — we've never seen an otherwise disinterested puppy turn down a piece of liver. The exception to using special treats is for the excitable pup that can't be readily taught to take the tidbit without turning somersaults. This pup can be trained with bits of his regular food.

We think that using tidbits is the quickest and easiest way to teach puppies how to learn. Their use, however, must be put in perspective. A tidbit is a *secondary* reward. Your voice is the *primary* reward. This means that your pup will learn that your exciting voice and playful pats are especially great because they're immediately followed by a favorite tidbit. Gradually, you will stop offering the tidbit, and then your voice and enthusiasm will become the pup's total reward.

Teaching the Tasks

Leash Training. When you first introduce your puppy to a leash, clip it onto his collar and follow him wherever he goes. Some pups adjust to a leash immediately, while others might need several sessions of just having it attached to them. The pup should wear a comfortable buckle collar — keep checking it for size, because puppies grow fast. The leash should be about six feet long and should be made of nylon, cotton webbing, or leather. A piece of soft clothes line will also get the job done. No chain leashes, please.

Teaching the this-way command is a successful way of helping your pup learn about walking with a leash. The importance of this exercise belies its simplicity. Don't shortchange it. Take it on faith that it not only teaches walking on a leash, it also reinforces and rewards your pup for paying attention and for looking at you when he hears his name.

Call your pup's name. As soon as he turns towards you, praise with a "good dog," call him to you with a "Come," and reward with a tidbit. *Photos by Jane Exon.*

Walk briskly with your pup on the leash. When he gets out to the end of the leash, say, "Tippy, this way." As *soon* as he turns toward you, say "good dog" to let him know that's what you want. If he ignores you, repeat, "Tippy, this way," then get down on your knees and coax him to you. This puts you on the pup's level and he'll respond more readily. If your pup continues to ignore you, give a brisk tug on the leash; always give the command before you tug the leash. He'll soon learn that he can avoid the tug if he turns toward you as soon as he hears his name and the command. When he gets to you, praise him and give him a tidbit — something wonderful that he loves! Then start walking again, repeating the this-way procedure as soon as he's at the end of his leash.

After a few times of "this way" in rapid succession, your pup will probably stay close to you, which is wonderful. At this point, turn it into a game and try to get away from your pup. Go in the opposite direction of your puppy and say, "This way." Praise your puppy, then give him a treat. Go in the opposite direction again and say, "This way." Once again, praise him and give him a treat. Continue this drill as part of the pup's training for two to three weeks. Your praise can occasionally begin to take the place of the treat. This leash training, incorporated with walking-alongside training, keeps a pup from continually straining on the leash.

The Sit. Your pup is accustomed to your hand, and you'll use hand movement to teach the sit. Hold your hand with the tidbit right on top of the pup's nose. With a wiggly pup, touch the front of his nose. Say "sit" while moving your hand back (parallel to the floor, not up). As soon as he sits, say, "good dog," and give him the tidbit. Don't expect him to stay there, because he's much too lively for that.

For the very young pup or for the pup that is too bouncy to put his tail on the floor, quickly give a tidbit when the pup's hind legs bend even the slightest amount. You'll be amazed to see a good sit in two or three days. One pup took a week of this before he finally would sit, but that's the exception. Continue guiding with treats until a snappy sit is consistent. As soon as your pup will sit on voice command, without being guided, give him a tidbit for a job well done.

Good hand position for teaching the "Sit." The leash is used for training in the park, but isn't needed in the house. *Photos by Jane Exon.*

When you are guiding your pup with the tidbit, praise the pup while he is taking the tidbit. When the tidbit is for a job well done, praise him first, then immediately give him the tidbit. There will come a time when your praise will take the place of the tidbit.

The Come. Your hands will be the visual reinforcement of your come command. To begin teaching the command, have both hands close in front of you holding a tidbit. With your pup right there, licking the tidbit, walk backward, repeating the come command. After a few steps, give the treat to the pup and praise him. A few times of doing this is usually sufficient to impress your pup with the rewards of coming right up to you.

Your come commands can be anywhere in the house or in a fenced yard. No leash is needed on the pup. Kneel down on the pup's level. Be sure that the pup is close to you, looking at you, before you tell him to come. Distance comes much later. Puppies learn quickest when they have success. Use the pup's name and then the command. "Tippy, Come!" Clap your hands or pat the floor, or both. You'll find that in a month or two when your pup is distracted by something, or you're farther away, your pup will respond to your hand movements when he was initially deaf to your voice. Always use them together in this teaching phase.

Gradually increase the distance from your pup when you call him to you, but only up to twenty or thirty feet. If he gets distracted, get his attention back on you, walking closer to him if necessary. When your pup comes all the way to you for his tidbit, touch his collar with your other hand. This helps him to be comfortable with a hand reaching for the collar in the future when you might not have a tidbit. Don't grab for the pup when he's close to you but not all the way in toward you. If you do, he'll quickly learn the play-around-just-out-of-reach game that puppies think is such fun.

A reminder (because we all tend to get frustrated at times) — *never scold your pup once he has finally come.* You needn't praise profusely, but you simply can't show your anger, because that's a sure way to teach your pup to go the other direction when you call. Try walking away; your pup will probably come just because you're ignoring him.

Now it's time to practice the come command in parks and open spaces. For this, you need a long line that you can buy already made, or you can go to a hardware store and make your own. Select a soft cord or a cotton or nylon leash-type fabric that is twenty to thirty feet long. Choose whatever will be comfortable in your hand if your pup, and later your grown dog, pulls on it. Buy a small clasp, one that isn't too big and heavy for the size of your pup, and put the clasp together with the long line. Some stores will even do this for you. A retractable long line, called a Flexi-Lead®, is available in pet-supply stores. This is absolutely the best for both you and your dog. It takes the pulling pressure off of your arms and shoulders, and your dog is always under control. Yet, it allows him the liberty of running, sniffing, and being a normal dog on a walk.

Now take your pup for a walk. Let him wander around, and when he's interested in sniffing and poking around, call his name. If he doesn't look at you, call his name again and give a quick tug on the line. When he looks at you, praise him immediately and call him to you, giving him a tidbit and touching his collar. Then let him run out on his long line again. Call him to you occasionally during the walk. This teaches him to check in with you (getting a tidbit) before going out again.

The Walk Alongside. Your hand is the guide for showing your puppy that bouncing along close to your side is a great place to be. You have two goals in this exercise: (1) to keep the pup's attention on you, and (2) to keep a loose leash. Right now, your pup's attention span is very short. The first few times that you practice this with your pup, give him a few seconds to pay attention — this is long enough.

To increase the length of your pup's attention span, train only while the pup is paying attention to you. If you go on too long, the pup will learn that it's okay to ignore you. You can, however, repeat the few seconds of heeling several times in a five- to ten-minute period.

Reminders:

• Work the puppy on your left side.
• Do whatever is necessary to keep your pup's attention. Let your

To begin the walk
alongside, the tidbit is
almost on the pup's
nose.

Later, the tidbit is held
up to your waist, and
lowered when needed.

pup lick and nibble the tidbit in your left hand. Talk to him and call his name. After a few training sessions, raise your hand holding the tidbit to your waist, then lower it back down in front of his nose whenever he becomes distracted. If he gets a couple of feet away from you, call him with "come." Walk backward, then give him the tidbit when he gets to you. Continue walking forward.

- Move at a pace to keep your puppy trotting or jogging.
- Stop while the pup is still paying attention to you. Gradually increase the length of time of each heeling.
- If your pup is pulling on the leash, you don't have his attention. A tight leash telegraphs what you're going to do so that the pup has no incentive to pay attention.
- Praise your pup at the end of each heeling "trip." Pat the pup and use a happy voice. If your pup is too excitable, just use your voice; the pats will come later.

The walk alongside is preferably done with no leash, but if you're in an area where you must have a leash on your puppy, fold it up in your right hand until it is comfortably loose as it hangs down from the pup's collar. If you have your puppy out for a walk, do this exercise a couple of times during the walk, then let the pup whiz around, sniffing and learning about the world, the rest of the time.

This is one of those tasks that gives your pup the right attitude toward staying at your side. It will be applied with great success when he's a few months older and you want to teach him a more formal heel command.

The Down Stay. The down command, followed by a stay (which will only be for five to ten seconds at first but gradually works up to a minute), impresses upon your pup his relationship with you — benevolent and worthy of respect. This is especially important for males or dominant breeds or individuals. For the down, put the tidbit right under your pup's nose (he's sitting), then down to the floor between his feet, and finally out in front. He should lie down as he follows it. If he doesn't, help him by *gently* pushing down on his shoulders.

After your pup has learned the down command and is comfortable with it, add the stay command. Put your foot on the leash, close to the clasp, and stand up. The pup won't be able to stand up because the leash is too short. If he wiggles, he soon finds out that he can't go anyplace, and then he lays back down again. He's

To teach the "Down Stay," put your foot on the leash close to the clasp of the leash. *Photo by Jane Exon.*

When the pup starts to move, the leash reminds him to stay. *Photo by Jane Exon.*

teaching himself that when you say "down" and "stay," he is expected to lie down and stay there. Don't take your foot off the leash until you have released him with your voice. "Okay, good dog!"

The second step is a down stay with the leash on the floor, but you don't stand on it; therefore, you need to be ready to stop the pup the instant he starts to move. Gradually work up to a minute in time, but continue to stand close to the pup.

The Sit Stay. The first step is to reach the point where your pup is comfortable sitting at your side for at least a count of five. You can stroke your pup, scratching behind the ears to help him relax and sit still. Do not attempt this exercise before your pup is twelve weeks of age.

Fold the leash in your left hand so that it is taut, and put your hand straight up above your pup's head. Place your open right hand in front of the pup's nose. Give the command "stay." Step

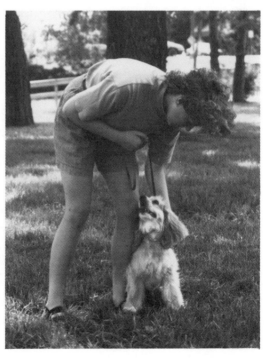

Some puppies are very wiggly and have to learn to sit quietly at your side before you can teach the "Stay." *Photo by Jane Exon.*

Mickie can now concentrate long enough to sit while Liz steps away. *Photo by Jane Exon.*

Puppies can learn to concentrate even with distractions for 20-30 seconds. *Photo by Jane Exon.*

WHAT YOU CAN EXPECT FROM YOUR PUPPY

Your training program will be in the everyday process of living with your puppy. It's *your* responsibility to insist on your pup's attention — your pup's responsibility is to be happy and playful in responding to you. To keep your pup tuned in to you, continually raise your expectations. As the weeks go by, expect the following behaviors to become consistent.

To concentrate on what he/she is doing. Begin with a few seconds of your pup's total attention while walking at your side, gradually extending the length of time up to a minute.

To pay attention. The Watch-Me is a good way to reinforce this (and also puts you in the alpha position.)

To look towards you when pup hears its name. Follow through with a Sit, or a Come, or just a Good Dog!

To sit. The control you have by using this command is basic to teaching your dog good manners. After you stop his/her bad behavior, insist on a "Sit." He has then responded to your authority and you praise him for good behavior.

To come when called — at a short distance off-leash, and from a farther distance on a long-line. Keep a few tidbits in your pocket to reward your pup when he gets to you.

To lie down and stay there a short while. This communicates your alpha relationship. Begin with 10 seconds, gradually lengthening to 1-2 minutes.

directly in front of your pup with your toes almost touching the pup's toes. Count to five, then step back to heel position. Count to three, release, and give praise.

A pup learns to do things in a step-by-step manner. For example, in teaching the sit stay, you must first teach him to stay while you stand toe-to-toe in front him, then to stay while you're a couple of feet in front of him. You must be able to still correct him with a tug on the leash if he starts to move. You then teach him to stay while you walk around him, and you must still be able to correct him with a tug on the leash. Then you work on the exercise while standing several feet in front of him. Many pups will take several weeks to progress through these steps, but they are necessary if you want to teach the stay effectively.

Then Versus Now in Puppy Training

The era of the small-town dog is probably gone forever. No longer does the family dog trot to the park with the kids, follow them as they move on to other pursuits, wander back home to cool off under the porch, and visit a few dog friends on the way.

No, the life of the dog is now much more formal and controlled. Because of this — because your dog no longer has the luxury of exercising his natural dog behavior, expending energy whenever his energy level is high and socializing with his own subculture of friends — you owe him a lot. You owe him as good a life as you can give him. You owe him play time and learning time so that you can live together in mutual trust, joy, and respect.

CHAPTER 12

THE SECOND SIX MONTHS

*Puppies appear to learn quickly — but then it takes a long
time for them to acquire the confidence to perform
consistently.*

There comes a day when you wonder what's wrong. Your pup
won't pay attention to you. In fact, he seems to be going out of
his way to oppose you. Well, nothing's wrong — it's just one of
the difficult times that a puppy goes through (difficult for you but
not for him). At six or seven months of age, and again around
twelve months, your dog will challenge your leadership. This is a
very normal thing for your pup to do, so don't get upset. Tell the
pup that you know what he's doing and that you're still the boss.

This is a transition age, beyond puppyhood and prior to maturity.
It's called adolescence. Male hormones are surging during these

months. If your puppy hasn't been neutered, he's becoming more intense and excitable about investigating everything in his environment. If a female hasn't been spayed, she may exhibit behaviors such as silliness and may not respond to commands that she knows. This can occur just before she comes into estrus as well as during that period of time.

During this portion of your dog's life, he or she will try your patience severely. Some go through another chewing frenzy around eight or nine months, or around twelve months. They have so much energy that they seem to be deaf and don't respond to your voice like they did two or three months ago. In fact, around twelve months of age, your pup can be totally exasperating. Not only does your dog behave like an idiot, but he may seem to be treating you with disdain. Don't panic. This, too, shall pass. Keep insisting on the good behaviors that he learned when he was young and cooperative. There will soon come a time when he's a good dog and is happily agreeable again.

During these months, the best approach with your pup is to keep training the basic commands and using these commands to enforce your good-behavior policy. An obedience class is an excellent idea, because it puts you on a routine with weekly goals. Your young dog will learn to respond to you even with the distraction of other dogs. But applying these commands to help your dog maintain good manners at home is up to you.

Use the Basic Commands to Control Behavior

You need an attitude of determination and a will to be consistent with your training regimen. You must insist on your dog learning good behavior when friends arrive, and on his using good door behavior when he goes in and out. You must expect your dog to respond to you and to be controlled when you're out walking and other people approach. This is where determination and consistency come in. You must insist on good behavior (without losing patience and saying, "Oh, it's hopeless"), and you must use the same procedure (consistency) each time you correct a behavior. If you can manage these two factors, you will be amazed that your dog's behavior actually does improve.

Reinforce Basic Commands

The sit command is one that you will use for control in any situation. It's an excellent way to discipline your dog in the sense that it stops his bad behavior (he can't jump or run or even bark much if he's on a sit stay), and it puts you in control and gains your dog's respect.

To make certain that your dog understands "sit" to mean "sit now," do random sits. Walk him a few steps, not on a heel command but on a "let's go," and give him the sit command. If he ignores you, put your right hand on the leash near the collar and your left hand across his back just in front of his hind legs. Pull up on the leash, and squeeze down and back with the thumb and third finger of your left hand. Repeat the "sit" as you sit him. Always be ready to use both hands to sit your dog if he doesn't respond to your command immediately. You can progress to using only the leash, tugged straight up, on the sit. Then he should begin responding to the sit without any cues from you. But *always* be ready to show him that you're alert and in control and that you will correct him instantly whenever he ignores your command.

Use this same approach when you're reviewing the other commands that your dog knows. You have to concentrate as much or more than you expect your dog to. The more you concentrate on what you're doing, the better your timing will be for a leash or a voice correction if your dog doesn't respond properly.

Insist on Good Manners

Now that your dog really understands the sit command, you can use it to teach good manners. If your dog jumps at people or at other dogs when he's out walking with you, tell him "no," give him a pop on the leash to get him back to you, and say "sit!" Let him sit there for several seconds, and get eye contact with a "watch me." At that point, you can tell him that he's a good dog and continue walking. Sometimes you will give your dog a sit command before a person gets close. Your dog can learn to sit there without leaping up until you give permission for him to move.

The sit command is excellent for teaching good manners at your front door. Some dogs are easy to teach to sit while the door is opened, but if your dog has developed a bad habit of barking and jumping and in general being out of control when someone comes

The Sit Stay reminds your dog to wait until given another command. *Photo by Jane Exon.*

Take advantage of any distractions to keep training your adolescent dog on Sit Stay. *Photo by Jane Exon.*

to the door, you might need the reinforcement of a squirt bottle with a dilute solution of vinegar and water (approximately one to six) ready to use.

Enlist some friends to help you by ringing your doorbell, then waiting patiently to enter while you work with your dog. You won't need a leash for this, because your dog will learn more quickly when he must be totally responsible for his own actions without being tugged and pulled on a leash.

When your dog becomes very excited and is barking at the door, give a sit command. He will probably keep barking because he's so excited. Repeat the sit command, and squirt at his lips with the vinegar water. Keep repeating the sit command and the squirt until your dog sits. You might be several feet away from the door by now because your dog will keep moving around, but just keep moving with him. When he is finally sitting and not barking, calmly and quietly tell him that he's a good dog. After your friends come through the door, you can release your dog from his sit. If he wants to jump up, insist that he sit again. Use the squirt bottle if necessary. Once you and your dog understand this procedure at the door, the dog will be more relaxed (as will you) and will sit without all the jumping around, and without being squirted with vinegar water. Nevertheless, keep a bottle near the door for reinforcement.

Another good use of the sit command is to have your dog wait while you open the door. You will step out the door, then call your dog to you. The same procedure applies when you come back in. This reminds him of who's in control, and it keeps him from bolting out the door or knocking you over to be the first one into the house.

The sit command can also be used if your dog is playing around out of reach and won't come to you. Keep saying "sit-sit-sit," pointing your finger and staring at him. Follow him wherever he wiggles or moves to, and you *will* get a sit from him. Now go to him and tell him that he's a good dog because he sat. This procedure reinforces the come command when your dog is feeling his independence.

The Come

A long line is essential now so that you are in control and can make your dog come to you even if he doesn't want to. After several weeks of using a long line or Flexi-Lead® and rewarding him for coming and checking in with you, your dog should be reliable off leash in safe fields or greenbelt areas. One of our students, Jim, and his Standard Schnauzer, was considering renting an electronic collar because his dog needed exercise but kept running off. We discussed the pros and cons; two weeks later he phoned and said that he didn't need the remote-control collar — cheese had done the job. Keep calling your dog to you, give a reward, and let him run off again — but don't let him get too far away before calling him.

The Down Stay

Practice this when you want your dog in the room with you, such as at mealtime, but not moving around being a nuisance. With a leash attached to your dog's collar, put him on a down stay (which he has learned previously). If he gets up, give him a correction. Put him down by giving a brisk pop down on the leash. Look him straight in the eye and repeat "Down, Stay!" If he gets up one more time, tie his leash to a heavy piece of furniture or other stable item so that when he tries to stand up, he won't be able to. This also increases his respect for you. "Down stay" means to lie down and stay there, with no exceptions.

Walking on the Leash

When you walk your dog in a park, or any public area, respect the other people who also use the park. Take some plastic sandwich bags with you. When your dog defecates, put a plastic bag on your hand like a mitten, pick up the feces, and pull the bag off so that the pile you picked up is now inside the bag. Carry a small paper bag with you to keep the plastic bag in until you reach a garbage container. If dog owners would do this, they would be more welcome in public areas.

Use the come command when your dog is pulling too hard on the leash. Call your dog, walk backward a few steps, and reward him when he gets to you. Now walk forward again and let him move along beside you. Repeat calling him to you whenever he

Every time your dog starts to drag you on the leash, call him by name to come to you. *Photos by Jane Exon.*

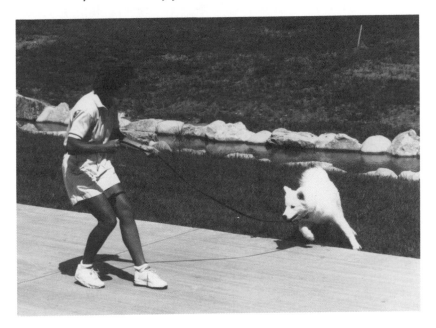

pulls on the leash. Using a Flexi-Lead® takes a lot of pressure off of your arms and shoulders and gives the dog more freedom and distance to exercise.

Behavioral Traits

Your pup's personality will continue to change during the next few months. Some behavioral traits don't become strongly developed until the dog is a year old or more. Traits such as stubbornness and extreme independence were undoubtedly hinted at during puppyhood but were very easy to ignore because "he was only a puppy," or because it hadn't become a problem yet. With puppy training, you have likely nipped many problems before they have become deeply entrenched. As the dog matures, however, you must continue to assert your role of leadership.

Other behavioral problems, such as barking or a lapse in housetraining, can be caused by stress or by a change in the daily home routine. Such stresses might include a stay in a boarding kennel or a schedule change by a member of the family who had previously been at home and then went back to school or work.

Some behavioral traits aren't very noticeable until the dog reaches sexual maturity, and then they can become obvious problems requiring attention. Roaming and overprotectiveness are some examples. The roaming dog must not have the opportunity to wander. He must be confined in a yard or house, or be under your total control when he's outside of his home.

Some dogs have a genetic disposition toward aggression or protectiveness, and sexual maturity accentuates it. Some dogs will just naturally try an aggressive reaction in certain circumstances, and when they find out that you won't permit it, they cease that type of behavior. When you are walking your dog on leash, any demonstration of growling or lip curling must immediately be stopped. An instant "NO," accompanied by an abrupt turn in the opposite direction for a few steps, then followed by a "Sit!" and a "Watch me!" should work. Tell him that you won't permit such behavior. You can now turn back to where you were. If he behaves, you can tell him that he's a good dog.

Territoriality

Almost all dogs have a sense of territory. Unless a dog has been totally forbidden to do so, he will automatically announce the arrival of someone at the door or on the property. Some dogs have stronger-than-average senses of territory and enlarge their area to include the route of their regular walks through the neighborhood. An aggressive male dog could become a problem because of trying to fight other males that are intruding on his street or sidewalk. The degree of a dog's protective actions is based on the relationship that you have established with him. If you have let him have his own way, the protectiveness will begin to show at this age. The pup will begin to put himself in the role of pack leader. This means that if he has tendencies toward overprotectiveness, he will begin to become aggressive if someone comes near his food bowl, or to growl at your friends.

Some people think that they want a guard dog and should allow this kind of behavior. This is not correct. It isn't necessary to encourage aggressive actions in order to have a dog that barks and warns you of strangers. Most dogs will automatically do this. A dog that is not controllable is dangerous to have around. Now is the time to get involved with a formal training program and get your relationship back on track.

Pros and Cons of Electronic Collars

The collars come in two types, the remote control collar and the bark collar. With the remote control, the collar has a small attached box unit which emits an electrical impulse when the handler presses a button on the transmitter held in the hand. The bark collar has a unit on the collar which is activated by the vibrations of the dog's bark.

Electronic collars have been developed into very sophisticated instruments quite diffferent from the original collars, but they can still be abusive when used by inexperienced persons. The use of a collar can successfully eliminate an undesirable behavior, but in other cases, time and money is spent with frustrating results. This is often because the person using the collar doesn't have an understanding of the timing of the impulse. In addition, the handler must understand the level of intensity of impulse the dog receives. In one collar, 15 levels are possible. Excess shock may cause the dog to be nervous or frightened rather than extinguishing the unwanted behavior.

Too many people think of the electronic collar as a "quick fix" for a bad behavior, which is *not* the way it works. Because of the high cost ($250 to $500), you might prefer to rent one for a week. But, even though it is successful, for example, in stopping the dog from chasing horses in the pasture, two weeks later the dog may begin chasing horses again. Many behaviors require consistent use of a collar over a period of time to totally eliminate the bad behavior, which means the dog must be wearing the collar and you must be ready with the transmitter everytime the dog begins the bad behavior. There are dummy collars that mimic the shape and weight of the real collar but a dog soon learns to know the difference. When used with the guidance of a knowledgable person the collar can be a means of correcting bad behavior in your dog when other training methods have failed, but remember, the use of the collar often takes as much time and personal involvement in training as another method would require.

The *bark collar* is effective because it works while no-one is home. Only the vibrations of the dog's barking can set it off; another dog's barking or a loud noise won't activate the collar. With many dogs, over a period of time (weeks or months) the collar then needs to be used only randomly, and then not at all. It is sometimes the only resource for a family whose dog's barking has become unmanageable. We find the collar preferable to surgical debarking. *Tri-tronics* in Tucson, Arizona has several models, some of which allow the dog to bark a certain period of time, but then prevent the dog from continuing on with hysterical barking.

Sexual Maturity

The indication that the female has reached sexual maturity is the onset of estrus, commonly called the heat period. This is not an indication of physical or behavioral maturity, because there is still much growth yet to occur in these areas. There is an apparent correlation between breed size and the onset of the first estrus. It generally occurs at six to eight months for females less than thirty pounds, at eight to ten months for females thirty to sixty pounds, and at ten to fifteen months for breeds greater than sixty pounds. However, there are always individual differences in these age groups. The total length of the heat period lasts about three weeks.

The male, at some time during the last half of the first year, will begin to lift his leg to urinate. This is usually viewed as a mark of the sexually maturing male and can begin anywhere from five to twelve months, or even later. Sexual maturity often brings on an increased attitude of protectiveness and an intense interest in other dogs. As we have already stated, you may have to take specific steps to reinforce your position as pack leader.

After the male reaches the age where he is leg-lifting, he might begin to do it to excess. Leg-lifting is the manner in which a male marks his territory. Many people think that they must allow their dog to stop at every blade of grass if that is what the dog wants. Excessive leg-lifting is often a demonstration that the dog has a strong tendency toward being the pack leader, and this is one way of telling you that he's taking over the job. In small breeds, this often occurs in the house. Leg-lifting to such an excess isn't necessary. It isn't pleasant to take a dog for a walk if he's constantly stopping to lift his leg. Therefore, during your walk, have a couple of stops where he can lift his leg several times. Then continue the walk at a brisk pace on your terms. The routine can be adjusted to fit the involved individuals as long as the dog gets his bladder empty and as long as you remain in charge.

Undesirable Behaviors

This is the age when young males begin to display behaviors that you might find very objectionable. Male hormones surge to a peak of nine times normal and then level back down again, which is one reason why this is a period of behavioral changes. Some males go through a phase of continually trying to mount other dogs. This is part of the maturing process and is in the category of play and trying new behavioral activities (which doesn't mean that you have to allow it to go on and on). Distraction is sufficient discipline for most dogs. If your young male has exceptional qualities and is being considered for breeding stock, it's best not to severely discipline the dog, because this could affect his breeding desire in the future. When your dog begins to mount another dog, call him to you, or use your leash or your hand on his collar to move him away. Then you can distract him, praise his attention to you, and give him a sit command with a piece of biscuit for a reward. (Don't you always have a few biscuits in your pocket when you take a walk, or even just around the house?)

Another disturbing behavior is when your dog mounts a person's leg or any other object to which the dog takes a fancy. Use the off command for your correction. Insist that the dog stop by using his collar and scruff for a quick shake as you pull him away. Then give him a sit command and praise him when he obeys your command and his attention is on you.

With consistent correction, followed by a command such as "Sit" (which is a behavior that you can praise), many dogs will keep these behaviors to a minimum. For the dog that continues to be extreme in mounting other dogs, or persons' legs, the solution is either to neuter the dog or to remove the dog from the stimulus of people or other dogs when he can't otherwise be controlled. A drug treatment is available, and your veterinarian can be consulted about this, as well as about the potential side effects.

Some males have the irritating habit of lifting their leg in the house, often in one particular room or on certain pieces of furniture. The smaller breeds seem to be more persistent in this activity than the large breeds. If your dog has a favorite area, keep it cleaned and deodorized. Dogs will naturally mark a spot that has been used previously. Another possible reason for this behavior is that your dog considers the house to be his territory (you just happen to live there and provide food). An obedience course can help you and your dog understand your relationship with each other. If your dog persists in this behavior, neutering is recommended.

Spaying and Neutering

One of the ways in which dogs can be helped to adjust to an urban or suburban environment is to spay or neuter them. This is *not* mistreating the dog or depriving him of natural feelings that are his "right." If the hormones don't send the message to the brain, the dog doesn't know what he's missing. In fact, it makes his life more pleasant because it removes some of the behavioral traits with which people find it difficult to live.

Don't consider keeping your male or female for breeding unless he or she is an outstanding individual in the breed and you are willing to spend all the time necessary to learn what must be learned before you can become a conscientious breeder. In addition, be willing to volunteer your time and effort to work in your community with the pet overpopulation problem. Many breeds have rescue projects that take a dog of their breed out of the shelter, do any training that needs doing, then find it a home.

The Female. There is no reason for your female to have one heat period before she is spayed. If you would like to avoid the problem of confining her while she's in heat, try to time the operation before her first heat period. If she isn't spayed until after her heat period, it's a good idea to wait for about two months, because it takes this long for the progesterone level to decline completely. If progesterone secretion is suddenly stopped, nervousness or irritability may occur for a time. This can be offset, however, by having your veterinarian administer a long-acting progestin. The behavior of the bitch remains normal after the spay operation, because this is the natural condition of the female between heat periods. A common myth about spaying is that the bitch becomes fat and lazy. If these should occur, it's a result of overfeeding and underexercising.

The Male. Neutering or castration does not change the dog's masculine appearance, because he will still acquire his secondary sex characteristics regardless of his age when the procedure is done. A study conducted by Dr. Benjamin Hart and reported in his book, *Canine Behavior,* indicates that castration doesn't affect hunting ability or watch-dog behavior. There are individual differences in how it affects other behaviors. Some differences are probably a result of the environment, but many are due to breed and genetics. Roaming showed the greatest degree of change, with more than 90 percent of the dogs having either a rapid or gradual decline. This is probably a result of the lessening in sexual drive. Fighting with other male dogs showed 40 percent to have a rapid decline and 22 percent a gradual decline. About 50 percent showed a decline in urine-marking in the house. The act of mounting dropped rapidly in about one-third of the dogs studied and gradually declined in another one-third. Much of this decline was in mounting people so that castration appeared to be a good way to reduce this problem.

There doesn't appear to be any proven difference in effect from castration before puberty or in the adult dog. In fact, some humane shelters and some breeders are neutering their pups by four months of age before they are placed in their new homes. Recent studies have shown no ill effects. And as is true with the female spay operation, there is no basis for the idea that castrated dogs become fat and lazy.

Well-socialized dogs are a joy to take walking. These two are six and eleven months old. *Photo by Jane Exon.*

Don't Worry — Have Fun!

During much of this chapter, we've been looking at worst-case scenarios. We certainly don't want to leave you with a dismal attitude concerning this age span of your pup's growth. It's a fun age, and our point is that many bad behaviors can be squelched immediately if you get at them as soon as they occur. If we didn't think that the rewards would be vastly greater than your training efforts, we wouldn't have written the book. Good luck — and let us know how things turn out.

Photo by Susie Miller.

AFTERWORD

You've brought your puppy a long way and have developed a good communication system. Now you can look forward to a long and satisfying relationship which sometimes will take more effort than you care to spend and at other times will have more rewards than you had dared to hope for.

If you have helped your puppy to become a good family member, then you have in a small but nonetheless significant way contributed to helping the dog become a better and consequently more acceptable part of modern society. In this event, we would like to congratulate and thank you for joining the ranks of dog lovers in our combined effort to foster good interaction between man and dog, thereby enriching all our lives. If we had a much higher proportion of well-cared-for, well-behaved animals and less of the wandering garbage hounds, the dog's image with the growing army of the urban and rural disgruntled might not be so bad.

ABOUT THE AUTHORS

Clarice Rutherford is co-author of *Retriever Puppy Training* and *Retriever Working Certificate Training*. A Labrador breeder and trainer for more than sixteen years, she is active in numerous retriever clubs, breed and obedience clubs, has competed in breed, obedience, and field events, and currently teaches puppy classes at a Fort Collins, Colorado, training center. Mrs. Rutherford obtained a B.S. degree in Animal Science and an M.S. in English from Colorado State University and was employed for several years at the CSU Animal Care Center. She currently devotes her time to writing and training.

Through her work in obedience classes, she states she has seen too many dogs living lives of quiet desperation (or, more likely, noisy and hyperactive desperation) — very little stimulation in their environment, and lack of consistency in the way their owners treat them. This results from little appreciation for what the dog has to offer us. The dog is a victim of abuse because of the ignorance of people. We have domesticated the dog to the extent it is almost totally dependent on humans — and then we abuse it by refusing to understand its needs in the sophisticated world of the 21st century. She is devoting her life to helping people understand the nature of the dog they live with, to respect its dogness (or wolf-like qualities) and in return, to become the alpha member of the pack and be respected by their dog. A relationship built on this respect becomes a richly rewarding part of our lives.

David Neil has been a professor in the Faculty of Medicine at the University of Alberta since 1986, where he directs the animal care program for the Health Sciences. This follows a decade as Director of Animal Care at Colorado State University, where he and Clarice Rutherford worked together closely on many projects, this book being one of them.

Dr. Neil received his veterinary degree from the University of Liverpool in the United Kingdom in 1959 and was in mixed private

159

practice in Wales and then England for three years. During that time, he came to rely heavily on the almost uncanny ability of the working sheep dogs, particularly where the treatment of large flocks was involved.

In 1962, he was commissioned in the Royal Army Veterinary Corps, where he first encountered the training of war dogs. The majority of the dogs were trained for guard duty accompanied by a handler at military installations, but specialist dogs were also trained for such activities as ambush detection, detection of anti-personnel mines and hidden weapons, as messenger dogs, and as casualty detecting dogs. Subsequently, Neil became involved in researching methods of protecting these specialist animals from chemical warfare when in combat zones. This work coincided with an extensive training period in the care and use of experimental animals in research, and ultimately led to a career as a laboratory animal veterinarian. This career raised many ethical questions in David Neil's mind and brought him face-to-face with the issues of man's use of, and interactions with, domestic animals.

He has been an active participant in the humane movement and was president of the Human Society for Larimer County (Colorado) from 1978 to 1981. At that time, he was involved in teaching animal-control officers nationwide. Currently, he is involved with the Canadian Federation of Humane Societies and the Alberta S.P.C.A.

Since the puppy book was first published in 1981, there has been a great deal of activity in North America in attempting to reduce the large number of unwanted dogs that regrettably must be euthanized each year. The authors still believe that the single most important element in attacking this problem is to do all that we can to ensure that people end up with a dog they can live with and share much happiness together.

PUPPY TESTING

Author's Note

To put puppy testing in proper perspective, it is important to note that it is only *one* of the tools to use in evaluating a puppy's temperament. The other tools are the breeder's continuing observation of each puppy's behavior throughout the first seven weeks, not only in the litter, but also when separated and spending time with a person; and third, a knowledge of the behavioral factors in that particular breed and in those particular bloodlines. The puppy buyer should not get hung up on the scoring at testing time, but realize it's an indication of the pup's socialization needs in the pup's new home. Dominance, shyness, and overexcitability are readily identifiable and are general traits that need special placement in homes that are willing to work with these personalities.

A Few Simple Tests

It's easy and fun to administer puppy tests, but it's also easy to form snap judgments as a result of the tests. Don't turn puppy testing into more than it is. It's an *indication* of the puppy's natural attitude toward people and a relative measure of the pup's submissiveness and aggressiveness. As such, it's a guide to what type of home and what kind of training will work best. It's *not* a permanent labeling of the pup's adult personality. One reason for this is that environment can play such a large part in the development of a dog's personality.

William E. Campbell developed a series of puppy tests which have become quite popular and which give a consistent overall picture of a puppy's basic emotional behavior. He discusses them in his excellent book, *Behavior Problems in Dogs*, and they are the tests outlined in this chapter.

The score sheet is one we have used for quite some time and lists the reactions we have found to be fairly common. The analysis sheet is a guide to interpreting the results of the testing and incorporates our interpretations of scoring based on observations of the testing we have done. Someday, we hope a controlled study will be conducted on puppy testing and its relevance to the dog's mature personality. Until that time, breeders who use puppy testing tend to develop a sharp eye from experience. They become familiar with the behavior tendencies of their bloodlines and with how certain reactions will develop later in adult dogs. They also can see certain behavior qualities that are not testable, such as that extra spark of smarts or charisma. Some puppies will have a reaction not listed on the score sheet. A pup will not be shy but will be content to observe and quietly do what is indicated but in his own time. This is probably an indication of a slightly more than average independence, or possibly an easy-going, quiet disposition. The pup should be retested another day to make sure the pup wasn't simply just too tired.

The test should be administered by a person who hasn't spent much time with the pups or who is a complete stranger and should be conducted in a room or area that is new to the puppy. These two factors are the means of introducing a puppy's reaction to a stranger and to a new environment into the testing.

Some breeders like to have the prospective buyers of the puppies administer the test when each comes to observe the litter, but other breeders prefer to conduct the test themselves first, scoring each pup in a litter while another person does the actual testing. This gives the breeder an overall view of the behavior of the litter, and this information can be helpful when discussing selection with potential new owners.

The breeder might be surprised to discover that a puppy's test score can be quite different from what his litter behavior indicated. A puppy who is very quiet, even to the extent of being picked on by the others, can score as an outgoing people-oriented pup. The reverse can be true also. An assertive pup in the litter might hesitate in associating with a person. Observation of the litter behavior with the other pups can sometimes give a false impression of the pup's innate desire to please and to adjust to people, so it's always advisable for a breeder to puppy-test a litter even though it sometimes might seem unnecessary.

There are a few simple guidelines: The puppies should be awake at the time you go to get them for testing. If you wake a sleeping puppy, the test might not give you a true picture of his reactions. It's also best not to give the test immediately after the pups have eaten. If for any reason you're not sure you got a reliable reaction from any pup, repeat the test the next day.

Testing a puppy isn't a rigid routine that must be followed in an exact pattern. Puppies won't let it be that way. It's simply taking a pup away from its littermates to an area with as few distractions as possible and doing the tests in whatever order seems to work best for each pup.

Here is an example of the way in which a testing routine might be conducted.

Come

Give the pup a few seconds to get oriented to the test area, then call the pup to you by kneeling down and moving your hands

Come Test

in a silent clapping motion. Be sure the pup sees you. If not, move and try again. (Refer to the chart in this Appendix for scoring methods.) After the pup has come running to you, do the stroking test.

Stroking Test

Pet the pup from head to tail for thirty seconds. If he bites your hand, he scores an A; if he just mouths your hand and is happily excited, he scores a B.

Notice that the difference between scoring an A and a B is biting. An A score applies to the very aggressive pup. All puppies have needle-sharp teeth and go bounding around with their mouths open, but the pup that scores an A actually nips you. That's his intention, though he may not be mean or vicious about it; that's his way of telling you what he thinks.

The Restraint Test

Next, do the restraint test by rolling the puppy on his back and holding him down with your hand on his tummy and between his front legs.

The Following Test

At some point during these few minutes, walk past the pup within a foot or two. If he doesn't follow, walk past again. Be sure he sees you.

Stroking Test

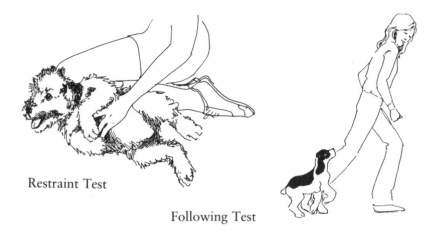

Restraint Test

Following Test

If you have trouble getting the pup's attention for the Come or the Following test, do one of the other tests and try again a little later. The important thing is to get a definite reaction from the pup even if it takes several attempts. If you can't get a reaction, that in itself should be recorded as a reaction. Give the pup every opportunity with the few minutes that he is in the test area.

There are two other tests for puppies that are listed but not scored on the score sheet. These can give additional information on the pup's basic behavior tendencies. One is the *toe pinch*. The pup that doesn't feel the pinch will need forceful training. The non-forgiver is not going to be a good obedience trial prospect. The pup that feels the pinch, yipes, and then forgives (licking, tail wagging, asking for attention) has a disposition that will be a joy to work with.

Retrieving a knotted sock is an indication of concentration and desire to please. Get the pup's attention by touching his lips with the sock and waving it in his face. Toss it about three feet away. If he goes out to it, he demonstrates he can pay attention to an object. If he brings it back to you, he has a strong desire to please. Some pups might have trouble concentrating at six weeks of age but should be able to by seven weeks. This test isn't for retrievers only. It's a good one to include for many of the working breeds.

Notes and Observations

Notes can be as important as the test scores. We can attest to the vital role of note taking. One author was looking for an assertive pup that could take a lot of hard work and training but that also had a strong desire to please. Her pick-of-the-litter selection had been narrowed down to two puppies with identical scores on the puppy test. However, her notes told her that puppy one had come to her on the first Come test even though it was distracted by a frayed rug corner. Puppy two needed three "comes." Her early records showed puppy one was the only puppy that didn't cry when removed from the litter and put on a cement floor at three and a half weeks of age and that was the most investigative pup with a rapidly wagging tail. This cinched the selection, but she never would have remembered if she hadn't written notes.

The puppy-testing session is an excellent opportunity for making general observations under conditions that are the same for all the puppies. What is each pup's reaction to you and to the surroundings? Is he generally very curious and active, or is he hesitant? Does he whine a lot? Is he easily frightened by a noise or strange object? Write down all the observations. It's amazing how easy it is to forget the little details when observing several puppies.

This type of general observation is a good way of acquainting potential owners with the pups in a litter who might otherwise not be interested in conducting the puppy test themselves. For these people, the breeder can point out the more cautious pups from the more aggressive ones and can also casually incorporate the Follow test and the Come test into the observation. In the final analysis, the selection of a puppy is probably more emotional than logical. However, it's best to try to place the pup in the home that his natural personality fits best. Many future problems can be prevented this way. A very assertive person will quickly lose patience with a quiet puppy that scores Cs and Ds (see scoring chart), and a shy person will probably never be able to become the pack leader of a very aggressive dog.

PUPPY BEHAVIOR TEST
SCORE SHEET

(Circle one item in each group)

COME (Attraction to people)

	Puppy #					
	1	2	3	4	5	6
Comes rapidly, nipping at hand	A	A	A	A	A	A
Comes happily, may lick hand, jump in lap	B	B	B	B	B	B
Comes slowly but willingly	C	C	C	C	C	C
Comes very hesitantly, or shyly sits and watches	D	D	D	D	D	D
Doesn't come, may look at you and go his own way	E	E	E	E	E	E

STROKING (Attitude toward social activities)

Very excited, bites, growls	A	A	A	A	A	A
Jumps and paws, happily	B	B	B	B	B	B
Squirms and licks hand	C	C	C	C	C	C
Rolls over or slinks away	D	D	D	D	D	D
Walks away and stays away	E	E	E	E	E	E

FOLLOWING (Desire to stay in a social environment)

Pounces on feet, bites pantleg, underfoot	A	A	A	A	A	A
Follows happily, underfoot	B	B	B	B	B	B
Follows slowly but willingly	C	C	C	C	C	C
Doesn't follow, slinks away or sits shyly	D	D	D	D	D	D
Doesn't follow, more interested in going elsewhere	E	E	E	E	E	E

RESTRAINT (Acceptance of human dominance)

Struggles fiercely, bites, growls	A	A	A	A	A	A
Struggles then settles, or wiggles the whole time	B	B	B	B	B	B
Settles, then struggles	C	C	C	C	C	C
No struggle	D	D	D	D	D	D
Wiggles occasionally	E	E	E	E	E	E

RETRIEVING (Concentration and desire to please)

PINCH (Pain tolerance and forgiveness)

*E in the score indicates a degree of independence. Three E's is a very inde-
pendent puppy. (Puppy should be retested.) Doesn't require a lot of human
companionship. Has very little desire to please. Training requires much repetition and patience from owner.*

*Note: The tests are not always the whole story. There's always the puppy that doesn't
fit into any one of the scoring categories. All one can do is score the pup as best he can
and then use observations to round out the analysis.*

ANALYSIS OF PUPPY TEST

Extremely shy			Strong desire to please in this range			Extremely aggressive	
3 or more exaggerated "D" responses	3 or more "D" responses	3 or more "C" responses with 1 "D"	3 or more "C" responses with 1 "B"	3 "B" responses with 1 "C"	4 "B" responses	3 "B" responses with "A's"	4 exaggerated "A" responses
Shies away for no reason. Retest 2 times to verify. This pup is virtually untrainable. 2 or 3 "D" responses with 1 or 2 "A's" is a potential fear biter.	Highly submissive. Will not socialize easily. Needs much gentle but firm training and confidence building over long period of time. Not good for young children.	Needs much praise and confidence building. Not good for an impatient person. Good with elderly and handicapped.	Good with children. Good for the inexperienced trainer, will let you make a lot of mistakes.	Outgoing & fairly dominant. Fits in most homes. Very people oriented. Very eager to please but needs a firm hand or will make a pest of himself	Learns quickly and needs firm, consistent training but not harsh physical training.	Contests for pack leadership. Makes a good watchdog. Can be trained into a faithful family dog with consistent repetition in training and minimum of physical punishment.	Will not socialize. Not good with children. Untrustworthy around strangers. Needs special training with very experienced dominant trainer.

*For evaluation of E scores, see footnote on previous page.

INDEX

Your Comments are Invited

If you found *How to Raise a Puppy* extremely helpful, or if you would like to comment on some aspect of the book, we would enjoy hearing from you.

Comments:_____

_____

_____

_____

_____

_____

For a Free Catalog

or information on other Alpine dog books, please write or call our Customer Service Department.
Alpine Publications, P O Box 7027, Loveland, CO 80537
1-800-777-7257

Additional Titles That May Be of Interest:

Owner's Guide to Better Behavior in Dogs and Cats
William Campbell

Positively Obedient—Good Manners for The Family Dog
Barbara Handler

Retriever Puppy Training
Rutherford and Loveland

Sheltie Talk
B. J. McKinney

Collie Concept
Barbara Roos

All About Australian Shepherds
Jeanne Joy Hartnagle

plus numerous other breed and training books.